# The Man in the

# Red Suit

Canada Council   Conseil des Arts     Canadä      Newfoundland
for the Arts     du Canada                                                Labrador

We gratefully acknowledge the financial support of the Canada Council for the Arts,
the Government of Canada through the Canada Book Fund (CBF),
and the Government of Newfoundland and Labrador through the Department
of Tourism, Culture and Recreation for our publishing program.

Cover Design by Todd Manning
Layout by Joanne Snook-Hann
Printed on acid-free paper

Published by
CREATIVE PUBLISHERS
an imprint of CREATIVE BOOK PUBLISHING
a Transcontinental Inc. associated company
P.O. Box 8660, Stn. A
St. John's, Newfoundland and Labrador A1B 3T7

Printed in Canada by:
Marquis imprimeur inc.

Library and Archives Canada Cataloguing in Publication

Templeton, Bruce
    The man in the red suit : a memoir / Bruce Templeton.

ISBN 978-1-897174-83-8

    1. Santa Claus--Anecdotes. 2. Santa Claus--Humor.
3. Christmas--Anecdotes. 4. Christmas--Humor. 5. Templeton,
Bruce. 6. St. John's (N.L.)--Biography. I. Title.

GT4985.T44 2012          394.2663          C2012-904659-0

*A Memoir*

# The Man in the
# *Red Suit*

## BRUCE TEMPLETON

### Foreword by Danny Williams

St. John's, Newfoundland and Labrador, 2012

*"For the last 30 years, Bruce Templeton and his elves have helped mold the culture of St. John's, Newfoundland and Labrador. "The Man in the Red Suit" captures 25 thought-provoking stories that remind us of the value of giving back, and how a single tradition and a single person can positively and constructively impact so many. This book could replace the 25 chocolate treats in the Advent calendar – the challenge becomes to only read one story a day. After reading this book, I am proud to say "'I am over 50 and I still believe.'"*

Earl Ludlow, President
Newfoundland Power, a Fortis Company

*"Bruce's memoirs as the man in the red suit was a heartfelt awakening on how the act of giving inspires joy for so many children and adults alike.*

*These stories have provided a wondrous reminder of how little acts of kindness can be so momentous in a child's life, whether they be with our own children or with a stranger's. Thank you, Bruce, for living the dream for all of us."*

Sheilagh O'Leary
Councilor, City of St. John's

# Dedication

In life, there are things you have accomplished that could not have been done without someone else's support. That is the case for me. Paula is a wonderful wife, partner, mother and now grandmother. She has been beside me for more than 40 years – when the times are good and even more when the valley gets dark and I feel alone.

While there are hundreds of "elf suppliers" who I can call when something is needed for a child, no one has been of more help than Paula. She is the invisible partner in all of these visits from Santa. She is in the helicopter, walking the parade route out in front of the sleigh and always quick with a needle and thread when Santa comes undone. She helps to anticipate the unexpected.

While there are many companies, employees, volunteers and friends who have assisted me in my effort to keep the dream alive for children (and I will acknowledge them later), Paula has assisted me in a *very* special way during this 33-year adventure as Santa Claus.

Thank you, Paula.

# Table of Contents

# Foreword

I have followed Bruce Templeton's career as a businessman and community volunteer here in St. John's for many years. His contributions on both fronts have been exceptional. Now, in this memoir about Christmas, Bruce Templeton shares with us one of the most important parts of his life.

There are times when we all have some big shoes to fill, but there are none more difficult to step into than the ones worn by Santa Claus. Bruce is the only person I know who rises to the challenge with the greatest of ease. Santa is beloved around the world for being generous, kind and faithful, and especially for the way he cares about children from all walks of life. Just as these qualities define the most famous man in a red suit, so do they embody the person who is Bruce Templeton.

Over the course of 30 years, our Santa has brought immeasurable joy to the hearts and minds of thousands of young Newfoundlanders and Labradorians. With the help of countless "secret elves," he has made more than 1,000 visits to charities, hospitals and other organizations around the province. Bruce has inspired a generation of children to believe that yes, indeed, there *is* a Santa Claus.

Santa has never wanted the public to know his identity, nor did he wish to receive recognition or credit for his work. Those were not the motives for this memoir. Bruce simply wanted to tell these stories of Christmas and share his heartwarming and inspiring experiences. When you read about his visits with children, you will feel the full range of emotion from laughter to tears, and the lessons learned will be priceless.

I know his journey as Santa has impacted Bruce in a powerful way, for not all of his visits were easy. His stories reflect this challenge. As you will see, the words of some of these children capture a sentiment better than the greatest orators. Their questions are funny, moving, and insightful in a very simple but profound way.

Bruce's memories of Christmas are meant to entertain *and* enlighten adults, because there is much food for thought in these pages. He makes us pause, for example, when he says it is "presence and not presents" that really matter. My heart was captured chapter by chapter as I read these descriptions of Santa's special encounters with children. Each true story explores one of the many unusual questions asked of Santa throughout the years. As adults, we are reminded that children can have a powerful impact in the simple but sincere way they talk about life.

As you read this book, you will be taken on Santa's journey over three decades. I promise you will learn from the children whose stories are told, and your outlook on life will be changed for the better. I hope all readers will be inspired by Santa when he asks us to do our small part to make this world an even better place.

I thank Bruce, on behalf of young and old alike, for sharing with us his extraordinary journey.

*Danny Williams*
*January 13th, 2012*

# Preface

The moment of truth in my busy executive life came while I was riding the Yonge Street subway in Toronto as it rattled southbound from Bloor Street. I was deep in thought. My work required me to travel for almost 40 weeks a year to cities across Canada and the United States. This was 1977 and I was part of a business team that had opened almost 100 retail stores in North America over a nine-year period. All of my friends said I was "successful."

At the time, however, I lived in airplanes, hotels and taxis. I left home on Sundays at 4 p.m. My children – one born in Montreal, one in Vancouver, and one in Oakville – were strangers to me as I ran for the Go Train or another gate at Pearson Airport. When I returned at about 6 p.m. on Friday, I would hear second-hand how my children were growing up. Thank heavens my life partner wanted to be a "stay-at-home mum," and the income we were making allowed Paula to devote most of her time to our young children.

I looked down at the shopping bag holding my new Eddie Bauer shirt as the lights flickered when we passed through the subway stations. There, on the outside of the charcoal grey bag, was the motto of the store chain: *"Never Confuse Having a Career with Having a Life."* I thought of my wife in Vancouver picking up the children from school, taking them to a fast-food outlet, and dropping one at swimming lessons and another at Beavers. (Or was the last event that I missed in my son's life his going from Beavers to Cubs?) I now had to ask an even more difficult question. Could "success in business" and "success in life" be two entirely different things?

When I got to the hotel, I called Paula. I trust her completely, and the best decisions I have ever made are the ones where I asked her advice first. We agreed that the time had come, so I took out a pad and started writing.

*Dear Manager,*

*I write this letter to tender my resignation. I thank you for nine thrilling years, but my wife and I have made the decision to return to Newfoundland & Labrador. We hope to find a more balanced life and to play with our children while they still want to play with us and before it is too late. We need to make some memories for us all; we are going home.*

*Yours truly,*
*Bruce Templeton*

The year after our return, my wonderful adventures with Santa Claus began. These are my short stories about extraordinary children and their families and friends. They are based on more than 1,000 visits spread out over 33 years. I was just a visitor in their lives; I came and went almost in the blink of an eye.

But as you will see in later chapters of the book, Santa is *very* special and he is *very* real. Children can see him, hug him and hold him – and he listens to them. Santa is a figure of enormous trust. There are no barriers to communication when a child is visiting with Santa, as I quickly found out on one of my visits.

"Thanta. Thanta." I felt a tug on my right pant leg. "Thanta, it's me, Anna. I'm down here." I looked down and sure enough, there she was. "Thanta, I have a question. Can you answer this for me? Thanta, are you God?"

Is there any sound sweeter than a five-year-old who whispers with a lisp? Her little face was beaming. She had curly blond hair tied back with a bright red ribbon. A Santa button pinned on her dress flashed on and off. I tried hard to answer her question (and similar ones like it as you will see later in the book). Anna is just one of hundreds of inquisitive children Santa has encountered. I have had some amazing conversations with children. Frequently, the visits start with a question from a thoughtful child such as Anna. This book is all about those questions – some more difficult than others – and my struggles to answer them. With a bit of luck, I get a happy response.

In the course of more than three decades, Santa (here, with the reader's permission, I take on his persona) has learned many things about life. Santa knows that children grow up almost overnight; we only get one chance to make memories for a child. So we need to create wonderful experiences for them, regardless of our circumstances. Santa also knows that it is your *presence* and not your *presents* that truly counts.

Children will love and respect you most for the special moments you share with them every day. It is all about love and laughter with a child; it is about appreciation of the real things that matter most in their lives. *What memories do you want your children to have of their time at home with you?* What memory do you have of your own childhood where you giggled and laughed at some very happy event with your parents, brothers, sisters or close friends? This book is all about enhancing a young family's Christmas experience and encouraging parents and children to engage in simple family activities they will remember forever.

For more than 30 years I have assisted Santa at Christmas with an average of 30 visits a year starting with the St. John's Downtown Santa Claus Parade and ending at about 10 p.m. on Christmas Eve in the Janeway Children's Health and Rehabilitation Centre. I have heard the questions and the exclamations when Santa arrives, and I am hoping that by writing about some of the true stories which I have experienced I will succeed in convincing readers that Santa does have a real role in bringing hope, joy and sometimes temporary relief from pain. This book is a collection of stories about those experiences. Some are very funny and some are very sad. In all the cases, the result was a story about a child I cannot forget. The question they asked or the situation they were in has made a lasting impact on me.

To help keep our focus on creating happy memories, this book is structured just like an Advent Calendar. I would encourage you to "open a door" once a day in the weeks leading up to Christmas. Together, I hope we can travel on a 25-day journey. Along the way, the central characters will obviously be the children and Santa. But I also insert a few details about St. Nicholas, through whom we have our Santa Claus tradition. I have enjoyed learning more about St. Nicholas, his beliefs and his ministry. Our Santa Claus is actually relatively young compared to Bishop Nicholas, and you will find out some fascinating things about him as you read along. Like me, you might find yourself wondering if it is time we gave St. Nicholas equal time, or at least recalled more of the old stories of Nicholas of Myra (sometimes spelled "Myrna").

I have also inserted some suggestions for creating other special memories of Christmas. One of them is a great recipe for making sugar cookies from scratch. When you are rolling cookie dough and decorating a cookie face, look at the child's face. I guarantee you are doing more than just baking cookies. You are probably making a memory for a child – while they make one for you, too. This is my wish: *I encourage you to arrange your priorities so you will be remembered as someone who cared and made a difference in the life of a child. Do a random act of kindness for a child. Then watch them smile.*

Throughout these stories, there is a message to the world at large, but one especially for busy parents and grandparents. I hope I can speak to young working parents with hectic careers as they rush around attached to their cell-phones, iPads and BlackBerrys. Perhaps there are single working parents reading this book, and they are trying to balance being there for their child or children and carrying all the challenges of work. The book is written for separated parents with young children, and all of the stress that marriage breakup can bring. And finally, the book is written for grandparents who may be fortunate enough to have their own grandchildren in their lives.

My present to you is these short stories of truly wonderful children. I hope they will bring a renewed sense of the true meaning of Christmas for you and your family.

*Bruce Templeton*
*Outer Cove*
*Newfoundland*

## Introduction

One night in October, more than 30 years ago, the phone rang. Paula picked it up and called to me.

"Bruce, the phone is for you. It's your Aunt Anna."

"Uh-oh," I thought. "What have I done now?"

Aunt Anna was my maiden aunt ("spinster" was the word we used back then). She was a determined force once she decided something. You didn't mess with Aunt Anna. My memories are of a smartly dressed woman in a business suit, with manicured nails, her hair perfectly done, and not a feather out of place. She was the oldest girl in a family of eight, which meant she held strong rank among her brothers and sisters. She was also a very successful business leader. So if Aunt Anna came looking for you, she had something specific in mind.

"Bruce, this is your Aunt Anna," she said in her strong and articulate voice. "I would like you to be Santa at the church Christmas party for the children in two months' time. I am sure you would do it really well."

I asked her if I could think about it while I looked around for an appropriate Santa suit. We did not have the Internet back

1

then, so I was left with only the local stores as possible suppliers. There I found flannelette suits and cotton-wool beards. I called Aunt Anna to decline on the basis that it was too big a responsibility to assist Santa if it wasn't "real" – and I had a very high expectation of what I thought "real" should be.

She listened to me and said, "Okay, if I make the suit for you, will you do it then?" As it happens, Aunt Anna was the provincial director of a very large craft organization. She knew more about fabric, sewing, knitting and weaving than anyone else in the province. Three weeks later, she called me to her office to present my "dream suit." It was red velvet with white lambswool cuffs and trim. A wide black leather belt with a solid brass buckle had been made at a local shoe repair shop. There were long white leather gauntlets which she had ordered from the RCMP, while the hair and beard were made of yak hair. (This is the closest approximation to human hair you can find.) There was a wide red leather strap with six sleigh bells attached and made at the saddler's shop, a big green velour sack with gold cord and tassels, and a red bag with the word "Mail" embroidered on it. She even had the long black shiny boots. She had also arranged with the local optometrist to make a pair of Santa's round eyeglasses to match my bifocal prescription.

"Here you go, Santa," she said. "The rest is up to you."

Thus the great adventure began. Over the years of my Santa experience, there have been many suits and many changes. After one parade, the local furrier called and said, "Santa, your suit looks tatty. Send it down here after Christmas and I will get it back to you before the next season." Ten months later, Santa's long red coat came back with gorgeous white fur trim and a note attached, *"No charge, Santa. Your Loyal Elves."*

Other elves have more onerous duties. For example, it isn't as simple to make a visit to a school or a hospital group as it used to be. Who would have thought a few years ago that today's Santa would be met in the lobby of a building by a volunteer holding a clipboard and a pen? "Here you go Santa, sign here," the volunteer says. I look down and recognize a standard Confidentiality Agreement. There is a paragraph that says I will never divulge the names or identities of any child or family members in the group I am about to meet, unless I have all of the proper permissions.

"And do you have an envelope for me, Santa?" she asks as I return the clipboard. From the mailbag, I produce a copy of a document from the Royal Newfoundland Constabulary (our police force), my Certificate of Screening. It is only right that the volunteers and the guests in the room I am about to enter know I have never been charged with an offence that might involve a child. I understand the reason for this protocol. I just wish we lived in a more perfect world.

But let's put those concerns to rest as we head off on Santa's adventures. First, however, you need to know a few of Santa's secrets – the "magic" behind some of his amazing feats.

Mrs. Claus is the only person who truly understands the logistics of the North Pole; only she shares in the busy life as Santa's trusted helper. We could never do it without her. It seems that you just get back to the North Pole for one year and soon the requests are coming to her for the following year. Setting the date for the arrival of Santa is easy because his first appearance is always the Santa Claus Parade on the last Sunday in November. The helicopter lifts off from the North Pole in the morning and flies low over Signal Hill, St. John's, and right through the Narrows of the harbour at 1:30 p.m. From then on, it is a question of scheduling.

A log of dates, times and locations must be kept meticulously. Most of the visits are held on the weekends starting about 11 a.m. and lasting for roughly 45 minutes. A BlackBerry and GPS device are part of my essential gear in the sleigh. Every file for a visit contains the name of the organization, the organizer and a cell-phone number to call on the day of the visit if there are any problems. When Santa leaves one event, he calls ahead to the next location to confirm with the organizer that Santa will walk into the room in six or seven minutes. Everything is carefully timed. If parking is an issue, the organizer has a permit and Santa is met at our vehicle. There are two (if needed) big green empty bags with gold tassels, which an adult takes into an adjoining room to fill with gifts. Santa then needs a washroom visit to brush his hair and beard.

There are other secrets to hosting a successful event. For example, Santa carries a two-way radio so he can transmit messages when he goes into a room. This simply adds to the magic. An adult from a distance can softly say, "Amy is on your left. Billy has the bow tie on your right. They both just moved here from Saskatoon." Then you turn to address them by name. Their eyes widen when you ask how they enjoyed their airplane ride.

Sometimes, there are unexpected changes in the routine for Santa. One year, all of the children brought a gift that they wanted Santa to deliver to *other* children. They were looking for nothing in return. The parents had explained how the elves simply needed help. If the children could make or bring something, Santa would deliver it to a needy child somewhere else in the world. So from that visit, Santa left with a large quantity of toys he took to families selected by the Department of Social Services.

Often I am asked why I do so many visits in a single day. The answer is a simple: it takes about 20 minutes to carefully put all of Santa's "parts" in place. This preparation includes Velcro strips that firmly hold the beard and hair in place, spirit gum for the mustache, prescription glasses, two watches, and the mailbag with a teddy bear. It is simply a waste of precious time to be sitting in a truck watching the clock when the first visit is at 11 a.m. and the next one is at 2 p.m. Waiting time could be *visiting* time, so we book the visits an hour apart and schedule them between 11 a.m. and 5 p.m.

Some of those visits certainly need more planning than others. In addition to the parade day, we use helicopters for several special events. It is absolutely magical when Santa is about to arrive at a pancake breakfast for 300 children and the organizers announce that Santa's chopper will be outside the building in two minutes. The little faces are glued to the windows as we descend in a whoosh of powdery snow just outside. Yes, Santa is here!

There is so much mystery about Santa for children. Most of them know that Santa has helpers; children see many Santas, in many types of attire. And creative parents also do their best to explain the multiple Santas. But if you ask any child in St. John's where they will see the *real* Santa, they will say: "At the Santa Claus Parade!" The Santa in the parade arrives by helicopter, has a long knee-length red coat, and he calls the children's names from the top of his sleigh. The parade is just the beginning of the adventure, but it sets the stage for all of the visits in the remaining 24 days. The children know the Santa they saw in the parade will be coming to see them. A room of cheering children goes into a sudden hush when the door opens and they see Santa from the parade walk into the room. "Look, mommy, it's the *real* Santa."

There is a special bond of trust between children and their Santa. On each visit, he tries to stay until every child has had a chance to sit beside him, lie on the floor while he reads a book, or sit on his back and get a ride. An intimacy develops quickly. Then those tricky questions begin to flow.

"Santa, there is something I need to tell you." Every Santa braces himself for what may follow. Or, "Santa, I have a question." I cannot come up with a good rationale for some of those questions. Who knows what might have sparked them? But I hear them and then seek the wisdom of St. Nicholas to answer them appropriately – because I know they will remember what we have talked about for a long, long time.

The questions generally fall into categories. First, we have the "practical" issues, and these get asked many times.

"How do you get into a building with no chimney?" (*Santa carries magic dust and Rudolph sprinkles it on him if there isn't a chimney.*)

"Don't you get hungry, and where do you go to the bathroom when you are going around the world?" (*Santa is well prepared when he leaves the North Pole. He always has a snack and makes a visit to the bathroom just before he gets into his sleigh.*)

The second kind of question requires an acceptable answer – even though it's important for Santa not to promise a definite outcome.

"Santa, will you bring me an Xbox for Christmas?" (*"Put that in your letter, Sam, and Santa will try to do his best."*) The critical point here is not to *commit* to something when you cannot control the outcome.

The third kind of questions are the tough ones that test Santa's skill and tact.

"Mummy died in a car accident. Will her spirit be with you in the sleigh on Christmas Eve?"

Or there may be another kind of awkward and heartbreaking question.

"Why does my daddy like to drink more than he loves me?"

These are the questions that haunt you. When you read about them in the stories that follow, you will see how I struggled to answer them and deal in an instant with these tricky situations. Sometimes you quietly tell an event leader that a certain child has asked you a tough question; most times you learn that the organizer is well aware of the situation, and together you search for a solution. You simply have to put the needs of the child first and do what is best for them. Prayer frequently helps, too! When I rest at the end of a day, I hope I have answered as if St. Nicholas was in the room with me.

I wanted this book to be a true account of my experience, so I asked various companies and parents who have helped Santa if I could quote them and/or use their names. I have done so where I was given permission. For reasons of respect, I have not quoted or reprinted any parents' e-mails that enclosed a photo with Santa where the picture was taken before their child passed away – unless I have special written permission. Similarly, when there were other delicate issues, I have omitted names or photos.

During three decades of Christmas visits, I have seen my share of life's blessings *and* sufferings. The experience of being Santa has given me some very memorable visits with children. While the great majority of those times have been pleasurable, some of them were very tough emotionally. I think especially of the visits to the Janeway Children's Health and Rehabilitation Centre. I have priceless memories from all of those experiences. They have changed my life. I receive much more from those children than I give in my role as Santa. I am constantly reminded during these visits that we are not promised a tomorrow. We need to think about our own peer group and what has happened in the lives of friends and family over the past year. We probably all know someone who has had a life-altering experience, and if it involves a child then the tragedy always seems so much greater.

The minister in our church and I have discussed the whole idea of Santa and the celebration of the birth of Christ. Today's Santas have moved away from St. Nicholas, the 4th century priest, but I like to think that my elves and I have our own little ministry. Being in the Janeway on Christmas Eve with very sick children, anxious parents and sometimes overwhelmed professional staff is also an important part of the season. I understand *part* of their stress because 11 months of the year I work in the financial services industry. This is the world of rising and falling stock markets, and the emotional roller-coaster it involves. It is a complete change to put all of those stresses aside for the three or four weekends prior to Christmas while I experience the joy of children. I treat that commitment as an enormous responsibility – which brings me back to Aunt Anna.

I will always be grateful that she started me on this wonderful journey. The suit she made for me was sewn with love, and it has helped to create a Santa who tries to spread cheer, laughter, and fun every holiday season. So bundle up and jump in the sleigh. Come and join in the experience of being Santa.

*Now, Dasher! Now, Dancer!*
*Now, Prancer and Vixen!*
*On, Comet! On, Cupid!*
*On, Donner and Blitzen!*

Chapter One

Will you help me keep the dream alive?

December 1st

Organizing for the Santa Claus Parade is a bigger task than most people imagine. This is an event with 2,000 volunteers, many floats and vehicles, as well as marching bands, clowns, cheerleaders, dogs, horses, and obviously *lots* of children. In a perfect world with an unlimited budget, we would build those floats in a central warehouse and bring them out on parade day. But in a small city, we have to work with many businesses and volunteer groups to create this unique experience for young and old alike.

We also have to be tactful in how we "manage" all of the participants. We are happy to encourage the service clubs in their floats, for example, but there must be "child appeal" in the entry. Otherwise some businesses might try to sneak in their delivery truck with a red bow and a group of children standing in the back of the vehicle. Then there are groups who feel they can turn this into the Santa CAUSE parade, and we have to say a polite "no" to them as well. Our goal is to bring a very large group of people into downtown St. John's on a bright and sunny Sunday afternoon to create an experience for children. It must be memorable and real. So, how do we do it?

The parade committee starts meeting in April and May of each year when we discuss new ideas for the event and decide which companies to approach. We know we need about 100 entries, so we start by sending float guidelines to interested entrants. These documents give the details about design, insurance, parade logistics, etc. For example, one rule states that nothing can be thrown from a float (even confetti), in case someone gets hurt. Also, candy or food cannot be distributed by entrants to anyone along the route in case there is a problem with food allergies. Commercial vehicles must have their logo covered, and every float should be in keeping with the Christmas theme.

After months of work, the parade committee meets for the final time on parade day at 7 a.m. in a local restaurant. If a decision is made to proceed based on the weather (we have an elf at Environment Canada who we really count on), then the calls go out to the media and to the city depot. Roads in the downtown core are barricaded, and parking meters along the route are covered with "No Parking" hoods. The radio stations then start the announcements: "Yes, Santa is leaving the North Pole in his helicopter at 11 a.m. and will arrive in St. John's at 1 p.m." About 8 a.m., just as a local television station starts erecting scaffolding, the city's road-closure employees are out doing their work. Any vehicles left on the road are gently towed around a corner to an adjacent street, where a polite note is affixed to the windshield.

A parade of this size is put together on a large parking lot and set out in ten cells, each with ten entrants. Each cell includes two floats over 20 feet, two floats up to 40 feet, one marching band, and two cheerleading groups with sound vehicles. Parade marshals check each float as it arrives by consulting the master layout. The floats are then lined up in order in the ten cells. On the day of the parade, we have city buses parked on the lot so the children can stay cozy before stepping into what may be zero-degree weather.

(If we are going to tell this story, the reader might just as well know *all* of it. Although Santa does eat breakfast at 7 a.m., he is *very* careful about his liquid intake. Once Santa is fully outfitted at about 10:30 a.m., it is a long time until 5:30 p.m. when he is back at his home base. We have to remember that he is 13 feet above the crowds on the top of a flatbed trailer for a long time. There are no bathrooms on the sleigh!)

The routine for this first day is always the same. Santa first appears at the Janeway Children's Health and Rehabilitation Centre party, where there are about 50 children in wheelchairs. They have had breakfast at 10 a.m. and Santa comes an hour later. Following the breakfast, these children are bused to a special area arranged in a parking lot along the parade route. Having met many of their parents, I know the kind of loving care involved in raising children with special needs – especially when this involves oxygen tanks, feeding tubes, or complicated medications. Every year, Santa gives away 36 special teddy bears to very special children. The bears have embroidered scarves that say "Santa's Own Teddy" and the date. "Elf 342," a local business owner, shares Santa's dream through her donation of the bears. Thank you MB. The first bear always finds a home at the Janeway party.

At 12:30 p.m., Santa goes to Universal Helicopters, a routine he has been following for more than 30 years. The pilots all seem to enjoy the flight, because we have permits that allow us to fly especially low over the city. Everything is timed to the minute. We know the first float leaves the starting point at exactly 1 p.m., and we know the parade takes an hour to pass by any one point. Santa's float usually leaves about 2 p.m. So, at about 1:20 p.m., the call comes from the organizers to get Santa airborne.

First, the ground-handlers strap Santa in with his seatbelt. Then they take the door off the helicopter, which allows the children to see Santa waving. Lastly, Mrs. Claus (a.k.a. my wife, Paula) is secured in the passenger cabin, although she is wearing her street clothes. After the chopper has warmed up and we have clearance from the airport control tower, we lift off with

Santa on the left side of the helicopter next to the pilot. We usually head out over the Atlantic Ocean before we turn back toward St. John's. This allows us to come in through the harbour at as low an elevation as the flight permit allows.

At this point, the parade is well along its route. Soon the children become aware that above them there is a real helicopter with a jolly man in a red suit − well strapped in − waving to them. The pilot flies the parade route back and forth until about 1:50 p.m., when the call comes from the ground for Santa to land. At this point, the chopper is put down in a playing field not far from the parade's starting point. Here we have to take some precautions. We do not advertise where Santa will land, of course, and we make sure the area is properly fenced. There are Rovers on hand from the Ground Search and Rescue Unit, as well as patrolling members of the Royal Newfoundland Constabulary.

Once the chopper touches down, Santa steps out and carefully moves forward away from the downwash of the blades. Then Mrs. Claus gets out, closes and double-checks the door, and then moves forward to join me. (For all the years we have done this exercise, we are always told we must never go behind a helicopter. We go *forward* where the pilot can see us.) Then we wave goodbye as the chopper lifts off, with the whole delivery lasting less than a minute. At this stage, Santa is escorted to the back of the parade just in time to climb a ladder and stand in his sleigh. If we have done all of this right, there should now be less than 5 minutes before the Santa float starts to move.

It is quite an experience to be sitting in the "big seat." The view from the top of the sleigh is breathtaking. Santa looks down from 13 feet above ground level. The lowest cable and telephone wire is 14 feet, which means these measurements have been made *very* carefully before the float is designed and built! Santa has a few minutes to attach a wireless microphone, which broadcasts through the speakers so all of the children can hear him. While all of this is happening, Mrs. Claus takes up her position. I know she has a small microphone and earphone under her hat. In her warm pocket, she has the transmitter switch. Soon I can hear a voice through my two earphones buried under layers of hat and hair saying, "Testing, testing. Can you hear me, Santa?"

"Yes, Mrs. Claus, we are good to go," says Santa from the top of the sleigh. Soon the big tractor shifts into first gear and the last float in the parade heads out onto the street. Santa is on his way. Each year I am amazed by the numbers. There are usually 60,000 people at the parade, all of them lined up six or eight deep along the entire route. The children sit on the sidewalk, with many of them wrapped in blankets. Soon Mrs. Claus starts her work. Through the earphone Santa hears, "On your left, on her father's shoulders in the pink snowsuit is Amanda, and her brother is Josh." A few seconds later as the sleigh moves forward, Santa looks left and down into the crowd. Mrs. Claus is good at what she does, so it is not hard to find the right child even in a large group of people.

Into his microphone Santa says, "Hello, Amanda. Hi, Josh. Thank you for coming to the parade." The expressions on their faces are priceless.

"Mommy, Santa knows our names!"

Almost immediately, I hear Paula say, "On your right, sitting on the sidewalk in a green stroller, is Jacob. His two brothers are Sam and Will." Santa turns to his right side to find the three boys.

"Merry Christmas, Sam, Will, and Jacob! Ho, Ho, Ho." The boys are wide-eyed and smiling from ear to ear. Their parents are delighted. Mrs. Claus is very discreet when she asks them the names of their children, and many of the parents now know why she is asking. But it is still a great joy to see the look of astonishment when Santa can name hundreds of children along the parade route.

One year, a child gave one of my elves a bag of carrots on which she had written, "Santa, for the reindeer. Love, Samantha." She had also written her phone number on the top of the bag. Later that night, I called her house and asked for her. As Santa's bells gently jingled into the phone, Santa thanked her for bringing the carrots to the parade. I told her I was back at the North Pole, where Dasher, Dancer, Comet, and Rudolph had shared the carrots with the others. Now the reindeer had asked me to call her house and thank her. Later, the child's mother called my office with the news that their daughter was up until midnight after Santa's call. The next day she couldn't wait to get to school to tell all of her friends. She will be a believer forever.

Many years ago, I stood on the top of the sleigh looking at the great sea of people along the parade route. I thought about the food banks and wondered if it might be possible to ask everyone coming to the parade to bring along a non-perishable food item. That simple idea has grown, and now the wonderful elves from Newfoundland Power push supermarket carts at the front of the parade. As the baskets quickly fill, the elves take the donated food to waiting trucks. Last year, more than 25 tons of food was collected for families in need. In addition, Canada Post collects not only the children's letters to Santa, but also more than $20,000 in loonies and toonies to purchase milk, turkey, ham, and other perishable items for the food banks. I am always thrilled by this kind of support.

One year I began to think about finding a new source of floats for the parade. Where could I find a work force that might help us build these big moving displays? As I drove through the city, I passed the penitentiary in the east end of St. John's. Think *inside* the box! Why not ask the inmates if they could build a float? Sure enough, it got started with one phone call. Soon we had the prison staff, the union, the John Howard Society, and the inmates all involved. They did such a brilliant job that the newspapers photographed the float being built in the days before the parade.

Young people pitch in each year, too. We give an annual Spirit Award, and one year it went to a local school. A group of children were on their float in the parking lot with Christmas boxes all decorated and ready to go. As they were about to leave the parking lot, the engine on the truck died. No amount of coaxing could get it going. So the kids climbed down and took their float apart. Then they carried the gift boxes, the Christmas tree, and the giant candy cane for the *entire* four-kilometre route. There was no question they deserved the Spirit Award!

After about an hour of constant waving, and with the sun slowly setting behind the tall buildings, Santa can see the end of the parade route. As the big truck comes to a gentle stop, a ladder is placed up against the sleigh. A volunteer climbs up to help get Santa discreetly disconnected from the wires and the radios. At this point, there are hundreds of parents with children pressing forward as Santa climbs down and goes over to the crowd. Then Santa gets into a big Rover Ground Search and Rescue box-style truck and disappears down the road.

Ten minutes later, a man and woman dressed in ordinary clothes emerge from the parked truck. They start pulling a suitcase down the sidewalk, heading to their car parked strategically nearby early that morning. Around them, families walk back to their cars as children excitedly recall their favourite float in the parade. The suitcase goes into the trunk before we quietly head home. Mrs. Claus and I have launched it again: Santa is back for another year. It is December 1st, and Santa has made his first appearance. We will be here until late on Christmas Eve when we go quickly back to the North Pole, collect the reindeer and toys, and head out around the world.

Yes, the parade is over, but this is really just the beginning of a wonderful month of visits organized for Santa. The stories that follow are only a few of my memories from the past 30 years, all of them prompted by questions from children. But it all starts with the Santa Claus Parade. With the help of more than 2,500 wonderful volunteers each year, we get a chance to make special Christmas memories for children – and keep the dream alive.

Chapter Two
Will you bring my daddy a surprise?
December 2nd

The phone rang at the "North Pole" in mid-November. It was the producer of a nightly live television show who was looking for Santa. At a meeting with his creative staff, this executive and his team had come up with an interesting pitch: Santa should come to the studio to do a live phone-in show in which children would speak directly to Santa. The idea sounded intriguing, so arrangements were made to have Santa arrive at the studio at 6:30 p.m. for a live show 30 minutes later.

A few days before the agreed date, the television channel started to advertise that the kids could phone in to talk to the "*real*" Santa from the Santa Claus Parade. This became *the* buzz throughout the city. Parents started to strategize about how they could get a phone line, be connected on hold, and then wait for as long as it took to be connected to Santa. Even the station's staff and families were suddenly jockeying to get a call in to Santa. Things were getting out of control. So Plan B was hatched.

Santa would simply stay on the set for two hours and let the hosts change at the end of the first hour. This was great for the hosts, but what about the poor guest? Especially under those hot television lights!

Fortunately, Santa has lots of resources, as well as some very clever elves. At 5:30 p.m., Mrs. Claus started to prepare Santa for his TV visit. Under Santa's long red coat are two big pockets, where she placed snacks for him and treats for the reindeer. Mrs. Claus also went to the refrigerator and got some of the blue frozen freezer packs that the elves use when we go on summer picnics. These were placed in the pockets next to Santa's belly, where he could immediately feel the cold.

"Don't worry, dear," Mrs. Claus said. "You will be fine under the hot lights of the TV studio. Just wait and see."

So Santa pulled on his long coat, hat, glasses, gloves, watches (one set to local time and one to North Pole time), and headed for the studio. The first surprise came when Santa realized that a group of children was there to meet Santa in person. The children obviously knew he was going on TV. Some parents decided there was no substitute for the real thing, so they brought the children to the lobby of the building. There was a crush of children as Santa moved into the studio, where he was met by one of the hosts.

"This way to make-up, Santa," said the host, as he whisked his guest down a long hall.

"We'll see you on the monitor, Santa. Good luck!" a child called after him.

The first stop was the make-up room, where an assistant came at Santa with funny round brushes and started sprinkling his forehead and nose with powder. Santa almost sneezed as the powdery dust flicked off the brush.

"Okay, Santa, you look great. Off to the studio."

"Five, Four, Three, Two, One," and then the floor manager pointed to the host. A red light went on above one of the cameras as the host looked straight at the camera. A teleprompter scrolled on a large screen.

"Hi, girls and boys in Newfoundland and Labrador. Look who we have as our guest tonight. Yes, it really is Santa! If you would like to talk to Santa and give him your Christmas Gift wish list, just phone him at the number on your screen." Very quickly, another monitor filled with blinking green lights, indicating that all eight phone lines were filled. The hosts knew their jobs well and the show began.

"Hi, Santa, this is Josh. Could you bring me a new Game Boy for Christmas?"

"Well, Josh, Santa will do his best. I'll check with the elves when I get back to the North Pole to see how we are doing making Game Boys. Josh, what does your little brother David want for Christmas? Santa knows he is only two."

Now this is where the show really turned to magic. How

did Santa know that Josh had a little brother named David? Thanks to modern technology, the names of children and their ages were there in large print on the monitor screen.

Sometimes children ask *very* interesting questions, so you have to think quickly.

"Santa, what is your favourite kind of cookie? Do you like white milk or chocolate milk?" Both are good questions, and they need to be carefully answered.

"Santa likes all kinds of cookies, especially Scratch Cookies, but don't worry if you don't have any. Santa has lots of snacks in his sleigh."

The show is divided into segments, each one moving along flawlessly. The floor producer points to the red light on the top of the cameras as each child is answered so Santa knows where to turn his head. During the breaks for commercials, Santa is handed bottles of water. Meanwhile, the frozen freezer-bags that Mrs. Claus tucked into Santa's belly are doing a wonderful job of keeping Santa cool – at least from his waist down! Then, about halfway through the show, the studio speakers quietly introduce us to our newest caller.

"Hi, Santa. My name is Emily. I am five years old and I want you to bring my daddy a surprise for Christmas."

"Well, Emily, that is a wonderful request. It is very kind of you to think of a surprise for your daddy. And what would you like Santa to bring for him?"

There is a momentary pause while everyone in the studio waits for the answer. This is live TV with a very short delay. Somewhere in a control room a hand is reaching for a mute button, just in case!

"Oh, Santa, I don't want you to bring my daddy anything. I want you to bring me a real pony. I think my daddy would be *really* surprised if there was a pony in our house on Christmas morning!"

The studio personnel erupt in laughter, while the host struggles to regain her composure.

"Well, Emily, I am sure you are right. I think your daddy *would* really be surprised if there was a real pony in your living room at Christmas! Have you thought about asking your daddy if there is a place he could take you for a pony ride? Merry Christmas, Emily."

The two hours go by in a blink. About ten minutes before the end of the show, the hosts announce that all the lines are still full and we cannot accept any more calls. Then the producer holds up a card that says: "Santa, could you come back tomorrow night?" Santa nods. When the host is given the information through her studio earphone, she makes an excited announcement.

"Children, I have some wonderful news! If you could not reach Santa tonight, he will be back with us tomorrow night and you can phone him then."

Soon I hear the familiar countdown to the host from the floor. When we sign off, a big round of applause erupts from the whole team. Then the wires are disconnected, and Santa gets up from his big chair and walks out into the cold refreshing air. Soon after, Santa is back at the North Pole having a cup of tea with Mrs. Claus.

Yes, it has been a long day but a wonderful day – all part of a simple mission to keep the Christmas dream alive for children.

Chapter Three
Can I be your bodyguard?
December 3rd

In many big cities there are community centres in the down-town core that house a daycare, youth clubs, and various sports facilities. In St. John's, a large building at a former military base at Buckmaster's Circle is used for such a purpose. This is the home of the Boys & Girls Clubs of St. John's. The atmosphere tends to be a bit rough-and-tumble, with lots of kids full of energy. You can imagine what an adventure it is for Santa to visit 300 local children at their Christmas party. These children are counting on seeing the "real" Santa – the one from the Santa Claus Parade. Santa definitely has to bring his "A" game!

Now, there are two ways to arrive on stage and one is much safer than the other. The safe strategy is to arrive quietly at an appointed time, find a change room near the stage area, and then show up on stage through a back entrance. Or you can be much more adventurous by arriving in full attire at the front door. In that case, you will have to get through a sea of clambering children! This takes a great deal of preparation *and* a certain amount of bravery – especially if there are only a limited number of volunteers. These helpers all do their best, of course, but we have to hope there are older children who have been asked (or who volunteered) to take their sibling to the Christmas party and supervise them.

When Santa is feeling particularly brave, he opts for the front-door arrival. The scene will be predictable. There is going to be a pack of six or eight young boys about eight to ten years old who are unruly and "cool." They plan to "greet" you at the door. Their hair might be spiked, there might be an earlobe or two pierced, and they think it would be cool to strip Santa down and expose him as a fake in front of the smaller children. Well, Santa is ready for them.

Under Santa's hair is a small welder's skull-cap which has been covered in Velcro. The beard has long straps attached to the cap to make it totally secure. No elastic for this Santa. It is so secure, in fact, that if a child locks his or her fingers in the beard and announces "You are a fake!" Santa can wince in apparent pain. Santa can then stand his full height and lift the child off the ground hanging onto the beard. That usually satisfies the first group of doubters.

As we know, Santa also has a headset with earphones con-nected to a wireless transmitter, and an organizer who knows each of the children. At this point, Santa can say, "Gordon, don't hurt old Santa. He needs to be in good shape for Christmas Eve to visit you, your brother Jack, and your sister Emily." When you start to name them one at a time, and you can tell them their brothers' and sisters' names, the school-teacher's name, their best friend's name, and even their *dog's* name, then you make quite an impression. At this point, the second group of non-believers suddenly starts to think there *is* something different going on here. Surely only the real Santa could know these things, right?

So here you stand, in the entrance of a very large building with hundreds of children racing around and not nearly enough adult elves and helpers to provide any security for Santa. Your instinct is to say, "I forgot something in the sleigh" and run for your car, but that is unacceptable.

Instead, you do the unexpected. You drop down on your knees making yourself totally vulnerable to the pack of questioning non-believers while you try to identify the ringleader. I take him by the wrists and bring him within six inches of my face.

"Gordon, Santa needs some help. Will you be my chief bodyguard? Santa needs to get up on the stage at the end of the gym, but first I have to get through this crowd of children. Will you and your friends be Santa's bodyguards and get me to the stage? I am sure I can find a small treat for you at the end of the visit."

At this point, something *very* interesting happens. Gordon turns to his peers and says, "Stop, guys. Santa needs our help.

He has to get to the stage and give out presents. Let's form a circle around him and help him out."

Then the magic unfolds. One the kids in the older group will have a smaller brother or sister, usually three or four years old. Santa reaches down to pick up the younger sibling. Most of these young kids are from large families and the young ones have no fears; they are not put off by Santa. I take off my hat and carefully pull it down on the head of the young child.

Gordon is astonished that Santa has taken off his hat and put it on his younger sister.

"Look guys, my sister is wearing Santa's hat!"

Halfway to the stage, you stop and lie down flat on the floor on your stomach. The boys circle you. Then they sit down cross-legged. Soon, all the other children gather around and sit in a circle. Santa reaches into his mailbag, takes out a big pop-up book with stand-up pieces, and starts to read the first page. "'Twas the night before Christmas and all through the...." The children all shout "HOUSE!" Santa doesn't need to look at the words as he turns the pages, so he can concentrate on the happy faces of the children. When the story ends, Santa puts the book back in his mailbag before he turns to Gordon.

"Can you help old Santa get up off the floor?" There is a rush of children who pull and push until Santa is once again on his feet and moving toward the stage. Soon the group takes you to the corner of the stage and you see the steps. A harried volunteer looks amazed that you got there in one piece. You turn to thank your new friends and ask them to come back and get you after the loot-bags have been distributed. In fact, they have never let me down. Following the visit, as I get close to the exit door, I turn to Gordon and say, "There will be a surprise for you and your friends tomorrow. You wait and see."

The following day, I call the event organizer to learn more about Gordon and his friends. I ask whether they enjoy hockey or the movies. Depending upon the answer, I purchase some hockey tickets or movie passes, which I put in a North Pole envelope with a letter to Gordon thanking him for his help.

Every year it seems there is a different "Gordon." In fact, after three decades, I have now had the opportunity to see these young boys and girls grow to be community and business leaders. (Even the tough ones who I thought were headed down the wrong path.) Truly, these are wonderful young kids. They don't really want to undress or embarrass Santa; they simply want someone who trusts them and acts as a good role model. They want to go home with their younger brothers and sisters to tell the story of Santa's visit to their community hall.

Meanwhile, back in the North Pole, Santa is drained. The jacket and pants go on drying hangers to get ready for the next day of visits. The big black boots get cleaned. The white leather gloves are sprayed with white shoe dye. The radio transmitters go back in their chargers. And Santa opens the compartments attached to his belly to remove the cold-packs that have kept him cool under the blazing lights of the stage. These go back in the freezer.

It's all about creating special moments a child will never forget. I know some children come from homes where it's easier to be tough than sensitive. But I hope Santa can bring a sense of wonder and joy that will be part of their memories forever. Is Santa real? Of course he is. Maybe, just maybe, it was the *real* Santa who came to the community centre and spread so much joy to the children.

Chapter Four
Did you bring a flashlight?
December 4th

We all learn new things about life, and Santa is no exception. Sometimes words take on new meaning, for example, when we realize how we might have misused them. Santa used to describe a child with a disease such as polio as being "handicapped." Then one day an elf set him straight.

"You need to change your thinking, Santa. 'Handicapped' means 'less than.' So when you have a handicap in golf, they add strokes to your score to compensate because you are not as good as the other players. The word you should be using, Santa, is 'disabled.'"

Santa thought about that for a while. Then he struck the word "handicapped" from his vocabulary when he thought about the unique challenges that some young people and adults face. Santa has the opportunity to visit many special needs groups, so he has seen first-hand that children can do some amazing things to overcome a disability. When Santa visits children with cerebral palsy, for example, he sees how determined they are to be mobile even if they have to rely on wheelchairs, splints, or crutches. There are children who have suffered strokes or brain tumours and whose behaviour has been severely affected. And there are parents and grandparents who know how these special children with special needs need lifting, feeding, changing, and caring.

Yet some days, even with the best intentions, Santa *still* doesn't get it quite right. He can forget about the unique needs of children who are less "able" than others. In the midst of a busy schedule of breakfast events, rushing off to a bowling alley for a Christmas party, or heading to an ice-rink an hour later, he can make a mistake. This was one of those days.

The routine for a visit has a familiar pattern, and being on time is a critical component. That is why Santa has two big watches on his white gloves. He must always know how long he has been at an event, and where and when he has to be somewhere else. When he gets to the next location (usually about five minutes before his scheduled appearance), he checks his cell phone for the number of the organizer. A quick autodial connects Santa, who whispers: "I am outside the building, but I will walk into the room in two minutes." This gives the organizer lots of time to get the children calmed down, be seated on the floor, and to start singing "Here comes Santa Claus, Here comes Santa Claus."

On this particular day, Santa had made the call, and the organizer said, "Okay, Santa, come on in." I pounded on the gym doors to make all the noise I could. Then I opened the doors. I shouted "Ho, Ho, Ho!" at the top of my lungs while the six sleigh bells riveted to the leather strap on my wrist rang loudly.

At virtually *all* of my visits, this brings the whole room to a standstill. But not at this event. The children just kept running, laughing, and apparently ignoring the fact that Santa had come into the room. Then the organizer flicked the lights in the gym and took out a big flashlight. She aimed it at me as I stood there momentarily blinded. Then she quickly turned off the gym lights. For a few seconds, all was quiet and dark except for Santa — who could not see a thing except for that very bright light. Soon the ceiling lights flickered on and now Santa could see that the organizers had the children's attention.

Suddenly a light went on in my own head! Of course, Santa, you are at the School for the Deaf! The room was quiet, but staff were busy with their hands and fingers as they communicated in HandSpeak or American Sign Language (ASL). Fortunately for Santa, there was an organizer who understood his new challenges during this visit. She took Santa to the stage, where she guided him to the big red chair. Then she reached for the big green sack with the gold tassels, which was full of presents to be handed to me one at a time. As I called a name, she signed it for the anxious children waiting to receive their gift. Soon we were happily in the routine of name, signing, visit, candy cane, and photo. The staff even taught old Santa how to sign "Thank you."

Soon, Santa looked at his two watches and realized he had to move on to other Christmas visits that day. Walking out into the snow, Santa thought about these children with their unique challenges. Yes, they are "disabled" in not being able to hear the sounds of the world around them. So they have to do some very different things in order to manoeuvre through each day. But equally important, we all need to find ways to help lessen those challenges for these children. Even little steps are a start.

Santa added "Learn how to sign 'Merry Christmas'" to his own to-do list that year. And Santa made a special note to remind his elves to bring a big flashlight for future visits.

Chapter 5

*Will my mommy's spirit be with you?*

December 5th

Back in 2006, some very creative people at the local Hits 99.1 FM radio station posed an interesting challenge for their listeners. *If your child could fly directly to the North Pole, what question would your boy or girl ask Santa?* The prize would involve making that dream come true for 18 children and 18 parents. (Thank goodness Santa has lots of elves!) The only requirement was that the child be between five and eight years old. And they had to live within driving distance of St. John's. Nobody was really prepared for what happened next.

Canada Post and the Internet got swamped. In fact, more than 6,000 families responded, which meant the station personnel had a great deal of reading to do. Over a period of weeks, the radio crew announced the names of one child each day until all 18 were named. The calls, live on the radio each morning to the winning child, were highly anticipated. (Santa got to pick a child as well, which I will explain shortly.) Fortunately, we didn't have to worry about the actual transportation to the North Pole. Provincial Airlines Limited (PAL), a wonderful Newfoundland airline with a strong sense of corporate social responsibility, had volunteered the use of one of their planes and its crew. The excitement grew each day as we got closer to the big trip.

There was probably a bit of chaos in some homes around the city at 5 a.m. as 18 children were shaken from their sleep, dressed, and taken out into the cold on a Saturday morning. They were driven to the airport by 6 a.m. so they could be met by the airline staff – all appropriately dressed as elves. The children (each with one parent) got their flight tickets, passed through security, and went on board the "Santa Flight" to the North Pole. The only alteration to the plane was that Christmas wrapping paper had been cut and taped on the inside of the windows. At 7 a.m., the plane was towed out on the runway, where it taxied and then took flight. After roughly 20 minutes, the pilot came on the P.A. system to announce that the North Pole was in his view. They would be landing shortly.

Meanwhile, there was great activity inside the PAL aircraft hangar. Elves were making their lists. They had arranged a long table piled high with gifts all beautifully wrapped. Very carefully, those lists were checked to make sure the seating plan and children's names were connected to the proper seat and row numbers. The clever elves had called the parents prior to the flight, so that Santa could have the gift of their dreams for them. If you

are wondering how that is possible, this was the North Pole and *everything* is possible!

When the plane touched down, it taxied to an enormous hangar. The big doors were opened, the aircraft was pulled inside, and blocks were placed on the floor to steady the wheels. Once the engines were shut down, the pilot announced, "Welcome to the North Pole!" The children were told that Santa was busy feeding Rudolph, but he would enter the plane in a minute. Outside, a wheeled ladder was placed near the side of the plane. A PAL employee then climbed to the top with a broom, which he swished back and forth on the top of the plane. The pilot came on the intercom again to ask the children if they could hear the reindeer on the roof.

Meanwhile, the ground-handling staff picked up two large boxes of real snow which had been brought down from Labrador (there was no snow in St. John's at this time). Santa knelt on the concrete floor with his arms outstretched and they dumped six inches of powdery snow on his head and arms. Then he stood up, jingled his bells, and with a hearty "Ho, Ho, Ho" he walked up the steps and into the plane.

The noise level dropped from high-pitched pandemonium to hushed disbelief as a snow-covered Santa stepped into the aisle of the plane. Children laughed, parents cried. Santa shook the snow off, much to the delight of everyone. Santa has lots of elves, of course, and so the night before this big event his workshop at the North Pole had been sent the seating plan for the airplane. Santa knew the names of all the 18 children, exactly where they were seated, as well as the questions they wanted Santa to answer.

Billy in seat 1B asked, "Do your feet smell as bad as Uncle Billy's when you take off your boots?" Annie in 3A asked, "Does Santa have a pooper-scooper to pick up after the reindeer just like I do for my dog when we walk in the park?"

There was a six-year-old girl named Kaylee who was seated in seat 7A. Santa had thought long and hard about Kaylee's question, because he knew it was going to be a tough one to answer. Kaylee's mother had died in a tragic car accident eight weeks earlier. In his letter to the radio station, Kaylee's father said his daughter was heartbroken. She missed her mother terribly, and she only wanted to know the one thing which – if true – would make her a happy child at Christmas. Kaylee had a tough question.

With each child and each row, I knew that I was getting closer to Kaylee. Then I saw a man sitting next to a beautiful little girl who was crying. She stretched out her arms and I picked her up. She looked me straight in the eye and said, "Okay, Santa, what is the answer to my question?" I gulped. The question was simple but heartfelt, and there was no room for error.

This is what Kaylee wanted to know

"Santa, will my mommy's spirit be with you in the sleigh on Christmas Eve when you deliver the presents?"

I looked at Kaylee, swallowed hard, and said, "Kaylee, you don't need to worry. Your mommy's spirit will not only be with Santa on Christmas Eve; your mommy's spirit will be with you for the rest of your life."

Kaylee slowly released her very tight grip around my neck.

"Thank you, Santa. That is all I need for Christmas." Her dad looked at me and bravely tried to smile.

On each visit, I have teddy bears with a scarf that says "Santa's Own Teddy." Sometimes, I carry more, as I did on that special day. I gently put Kaylee back in her seat and I gave her Santa's Own Teddy. I shook hands with her dad as a tear rolled down his cheek. I blinked myself, hoping the tears would flow into my beard. I knew I had to hold it together because there was one more challenge for me.

I mentioned earlier that there were 18 children. The radio station had selected 17, but Santa got to pick one, too. That was Santa's "fee" for his visit with the children. We had called the Janeway to ask that they select a child for whom this might sadly be the child's last Christmas. That little girl was on the plane in row 9. She had an inoperable tumour, but no one else was told about her health, and even Santa only learned later about the seriousness of her condition. The encounter on the plane that day will stay with me forever.

Soon the pilot was back on the intercom telling the kids that Santa had to finish feeding the reindeer. We also needed time for the elves to finish distributing gifts to some very surprised children. "Santa got my letter, mummy! Look what he gave me!"

Santa waved goodbye, the door was closed, and the tractor pushed the plane out onto the tarmac for its flight back to St. John's. As I watched it take off, I marveled at how we get opportunities every day to make special memories for a child. And this day, an incredible group of people had all come together to keep the dream alive for children. They will never forget their experience.

As for Santa, I still have a photo taken with Kaylee in row 7. I will remember her question for a long, long time.

The Christmas Tradition of Santa Claus
Part One

It is hard to imagine Christmas without thinking about a host of traditions that we usually take for granted: holidays, family get-togethers, gifts, and, of course, Santa Claus. But the jolly fellow with the big beard and the red suit is actually a fairly recent "invention." A much longer tradition is based on the life of St. Nicholas, and that story goes back almost 2000 years.

Nicholas was born in 280 A.D. in the eastern European city of Myra, a place that is now known as Demre. It is located about 45 kilometres from Istanbul in Turkey. Nicholas's name is interesting because it comes from two Greek words: "niki" means victory, and "laos" means people. So his name literally means "one who is victorious with the people." Bishop Nicholas apparently knew a lot about struggles, because history books tell us he suffered for his faith. He was a devout Christian who fasted, prayed, and did good works. Today he is known as the patron saint of seafarers, so he is often portrayed by artists standing with a vigil lamp to guide sailors on their journeys.

Other depictions of St. Nicholas – some of them in stained glass windows in churches – show him with three bags of coins. Apparently he inherited his parents' wealth when they passed away when Nicholas was still a young boy. And this is where we start to pick up the threads of the modern Christmas. Not

surprisingly, Nicholas was a generous person, as would befit a holy man of his time. He believed in sharing his wealth.

One of the early stories about Nicholas tells of a common man with three daughters. They were very poor, which meant they had no dowry (what we might now call "assets"). At this point in history, a woman needed a dowry to attract a potential husband. Otherwise, she was likely to be abandoned. According to the story, one night Nicholas tossed a bag of gold through the open window of their house. The man thanked God for their good fortune, because the first daughter was able to marry. Later, Nicholas made a similar gesture, and the second daughter was able to marry. On the night when the father heard a third bag of gold hit the floor, he raced after the generous donor and caught up with St. Nicholas. The saint swore him to secrecy, but the amazing story was soon being told far and wide.

Chapter Six
Do you only go to houses where
you get milk and cookies?
December 6th

There is nothing like a visit to an elementary school to re-mind Santa about the joy of the holiday season. It is magical to walk into a gymnasium or hall filled with 300 children ages five to nine. At age five, these little angels are probably still be-lievers in Santa. At age seven, there are those who question what's going on. And by the age of nine, there are some skeptics who confront Santa in public and are determined to expose him as a fake in front of their friends.

One year I got a call from someone who asked if I was the man who "played Santa." My response was, "No, I don't *play* Santa, but I know how to contact him. What can I help you with?"

The caller was a principal from an elementary school located in an area where I knew there were children from families with single parents and modest incomes. This particular school was very involved with the School Lunch Program supported by our community. These factors all related to the phone call. The principal said that a child of eight had asked her teacher a simple and direct question. "Mummy says there is no money for milk and cookies. Does Santa only go to the houses where he gets milk and cookies?" The school, in turn, was asking Santa to come and answer that tricky question.

Fortunately, Santa has some amazing elves. The first call was to Rotary friends who I know support the school. The club president began by contacting the principal's office to make plans for the visit. The next step was more complicated. There are privacy laws concerning what kinds of questions can be asked about school children (and for good reason). The school cannot answer some of them, but it was properly conveyed to the Rotarians that this particular child did indeed come from a home where Christmas celebrations – including a big dinner – might be a challenge for the parents.

At this point, Santa called one of his elf supporters who chaired a community support fund set up by employees of the local Exxon office. Within an hour, we got a call to say that a cheque made out to the Rotary Club would provide the funds to make sure a little girl's wish would come true. Then other Rotary elves went to work. One of them called a wonderful delicatessen on Water Street where Elf Janet (the owner) was asked if she could bake 300 peanut-free cookies and package them up for a special event. Another call went to Elf Steve at Central Dairies, who arranged for the delivery of 300 containers of milk. All of these donations were pulled together by a Rotary team and taken to the school for the final assembly prior to Christmas.

It was a snowy Friday morning when Santa and his Rotary elves all arrived at the elementary school. The children were already in the gymnasium, with the final assembly well underway. When Santa was finally told it was time to go in, there were cheers and laughter as the room erupted with excitement. Lots of little red-and-white hats bobbed in the crowd, while the school choir belted out a raucous version of "Here Comes Santa Claus."

Many years ago, it would have been fine if the children rushed to Santa as he came in the door. He would get his hat pulled off, or his beard tugged, although none of that used to be a problem. He could lie down on the floor while kids climbed all over him. Or he would give pony rides to those who wanted to jump on Santa's back. But things are not as simple now, because one of the big issues in schools is bullying. Children are now encouraged to be gentle with each other, and definitely with a guest as special as Santa Claus.

The new routine is that Santa visits each classroom *following* the assembly. This means he only has to deal with 20 or 30 children of the same age, rather than several hundred. There are still moments of pandemonium, but mostly things are orderly as conscientious teachers try to keep their charges under control.

So, with the assembly ended, Santa starts on the rounds of the classrooms. The kindergarten children are sweet, and Santa sits on the floor and reads them a story. Several who start out quite timidly wind up sitting on Santa's knee as the visit moves along. About 30 minutes later, we have worked our way up to Grade Three. This is the class where Abigail asked the famous question about milk and cookies. I go into the room and spot the little girl with the red blouse and green pants.

"Hello, Abigail," I say. "Merry Christmas. Santa has a special present for you." I reach into my mailbag and take out one of the special bears with scarves that say "Santa's Own Teddy."

"Abigail, this is Santa's Own Teddy, and I would like you to take it home." Her eyes are as wide as saucers as she clutches the bear.

"And as you are leaving school today, children, there will be another present waiting for all of you at the front door," says Santa as he turns to go to the last class of Grade Five students.

If there are going to be doubters and skeptics, it is going to be in Grade Five. So, from another pocket, I take a small transmitter and give it to the principal who is walking beside me in the hall. We have a short discussion. Then she stays in the doorway where she can see the children as Santa walks into the room. A young man comes straight up to me and says in a loud voice: "If you are so smart, what is my name?"

Santa looks him straight in the face, leans forward, and says, "Peter, your sister Annie in Grade Two told me you didn't believe in Santa, and I told her I would set you straight."

Then Santa turns to the girl standing next to Peter and says, "Karen, you believe in Santa don't you?" Santa turns to Susan on Peter's other side and Santa says, "Susan, I got your letter and yes, you will probably have a baby brother before Christmas." At this point, Peter turns to Susan and Karen. Karen is the first to speak.

"See, Peter, I told you. This is the real Santa from the Santa Claus Parade."

All Peter can say is, "Santa, thank you for coming to our school."

Santa waves goodbye to the class just as the final bell sounds and the children start to put on their coats. As they stream out the doors and into buses and the occasional car, my Rotary friends give milk and cookies to every child. And as Santa is about to go back into the building to get ready for his trip back to the North Pole, a grateful mother comes over and gives Santa a little peck on the cheek.

"I don't know what happened in there, Santa, but Peter says he met the *real* Santa."

Yes, Peter, there *is* a Santa. But he couldn't be Santa without a *lot* of help. Thank you to the principal, who speaks softly into the transmitter. Thank you to the technicians at Bell Aliant who have Santa wired with very small receivers in his ears. And a big thank you to my Rotary elves who live and practice "Service Above Self."

Together, we keep the dream alive, year after wonderful year.

*Chapter Seven*
*Would you like to share my teddy?*
*December 7th*

C hildren are unique, and so is each of Santa's visits. It is almost impossible to predict what might happen in any situation. There are always surprises – and sometimes these are eye-opening experiences for Santa. I remember one December day that was a real study in contrasts. There is a country club outside St. John's where Santa visits the children of the members. Santa usually arrives at this party by helicopter in order to save time between visits, and sometimes he arrives by horse and sleigh in the snow if this can be arranged.

On one busy Sunday, Santa arranged to have a second gift-bag ready at the second visit when he got there because he knew the timing would be tight. So, at the country club, the helicopter lands, the engine shuts down, and Santa emerges in the snow. As the chopper touches down, little faces are glued to the country club window in awe. When Santa gets to the front door, an elf is waiting with the presents in his big sack and together they make their way into the building with the children.

Inside the warm room, Santa's glasses fog over, so he takes them off and gives them a good cleaning. He spots a confident little girl who seems quite friendly and he picks her up. Then he takes off his hat and puts it on the child. Mothers and dads laugh with delight as the flash-cameras record the moment. Santa notes that the dress worn by the child is identical to that worn by her mother. Obviously a lot of thought has gone into planning for the party.

Slowly, Santa makes his way to the big chair near the Christmas tree, sits down, and the children crowd around. Then he opens the bag and starts to read the children's names. About halfway through the sack, Santa feels a plush teddy bear and pulls it out. Next on his list is a child we will call Melissa, so he calls her name to come forward. He hands her the bear, expecting a happy response. Instead, he gets a surprise.

"I don't want it, Santa. I have three of them at home." Santa is a bit taken aback, but he finds another gift in the green bag that seems to be acceptable. Soon the party comes to a close and Santa is on his way to his next visit.

Now he is at the Janeway Children's Health and Rehabilitation Centre, which is another world apart from the country club. As you enter the building, you notice the wide doors to allow for wheelchairs. Little children walk with crutches, while other children struggle with braces on their legs. As soon as Santa gets to the visiting room, he shouts "Ho, Ho, Ho" and lies down on the tile floor. The children are asked to sit in a horseshoe shape while Santa takes out his book and reads *'Twas the Night Before Christmas.* Then a big green bag is once again dragged into the room by an elf so that Santa can start calling out the children's names.

I look at the list and I see the name "Melissa" again. My mind flashes back to the awkward scene just 20 minutes before. I call out her name. When I look around the room, I see a three-year-old get to her feet and timidly come forward. I reach down in the bag and pull out something soft. It is a teddy bear identical to the one from my last stop. This little girl holds out two stumps to take the bear. Her arms have both been amputated below the elbows. I watch her turn and go back to her place to sit with the bear. Then she turns to her friend, also an amputee, and both of them begin to talk to the bear.

Back at the North Pole later that night, I tell Mrs. Claus about my day's experiences. I recount the story of the two girls named "Melissa."

"Maybe you should introduce them," says Mrs. Claus.

## Chapter Eight
### What kind of cookies do you like, Santa?
### December 8th

There is something quite magical when Santa is lying on the floor in a Grade One class surrounded by children while he reads *Twas the Night before Christmas*. The parents and teachers watch in awe at the joyful interaction unfolding with a total stranger in a big red suit. Some children rest their chins on their hands with their elbows on the floor. Others climb on Santa's back and take off his hat. Then together they mouth the words as Santa concludes: *"And I heard him exclaim as he drove out of sight; 'Merry Christmas to all and to all a Good Night!'"* Then Santa turns to the children and asks for their help to get him up off the floor. With great pushing and straining, the children get Santa into the big red chair.

"Now, girls and boys, before I go back to the North Pole, do you have any questions for Santa?" Hands shoot up politely, followed by a bevy of questions.

"Why is Rudolph the only one with a red nose?"

"Does Mrs. Claus ever go in the sleigh with you?"

"What is your favourite kind of cookie, Santa?"

That last one, asked by an inquisitive little girl, is actually new for me. So I pause for a moment before I answer.

"Santa really likes homemade Scratch Cookies." Then Santa concludes his visit and waves goodbye. Back at the North Pole later that day, there is a message left with one of the elves that a mother has called to ask if Santa would please send his recipe for homemade Scratch Cookies. Her daughter has arrived home from school and announced that she wants to make the special cookies she is going to leave for Santa, Mrs. Claus, and the elves. Here is that recipe.

First, decide on the date and time when you and a child will make Santa's homemade Scratch Cookies. The project will take either a full morning or an afternoon. When that date arrives and you are ready to start baking, please remember to reach for your cell phone, BlackBerry, or any other personal communication device and turn it off. Santa encourages you to "put your mind where your body is" – because you are about to make more than cookies with a child.

It's a good idea to read the recipe out loud with your child and then ask them to help write a grocery list. When you go to the supermarket or corner store with them, they can also help by putting the ingredients into the cart and bringing them home. For this recipe you and your child will need all-purpose flour,

baking powder, salt, unsalted butter, shortening, granulated sugar, eggs, vanilla, lemon, milk and sprinkles. (Now, you may be thinking, why can't I just buy a mix and add water? No, these are Santa's homemade *Scratch* Cookies. In fact, maybe Memory Cookies would be a better name.)

When you bring all the ingredients home, you will also need a measuring cup, measuring spoons, a bowl, cookie sheet, parchment paper, a rolling pin, a mixer, and some cookie-cutter shapes. Now it's time to get out two aprons, wash your hands, and prepare to have fun. Part of that fun will come halfway through the project. Once the cookie dough is made, the instructions call for the dough to "rest" in a refrigerator for an hour.

*That hour is Santa's precious gift for you.* This is special time you can spend with your child. You could read a book together. Go for a walk. If there's snow outside, you could build a snowman. All Santa would ask is that you do not turn on the television, and do not turn on your phone.

Okay, now it's time to make those cookies!

## Santa's Homemade Scratch Cookies (Memory Cookies)

### Ingredients:

| | |
|---|---|
| 1/4 cup unsalted butter | 1 tbsp. milk |
| 1/4 cup shortening | 1 3/4 cups all-purpose flour |
| 3/4 cup sugar | 1/8 tsp. salt |
| 1 egg | 1/4 tsp. baking powder |
| 1/2 tsp. vanilla | Optional: finely grated lemon and orange zest (about 1/2 tsp.) |

### Instructions:

Cream the butter and shortening, then gradually add the sugar, beating until light. Add the egg, vanilla, and milk. In a separate bowl, mix together the flour, salt, and baking powder, then add to the first mixture and mix well. Wrap in plastic and refrigerate for one hour.

### Shaping Options:

*1) Roll out the dough on a well-floured board and cut out the shapes. Sprinkle with sugar or decorate using the options suggested below.*

*2) Or, by teaspoonful, roll into small balls and press down by hand or with the bottom of a glass dipped in sugar. Try to make the cookies about ¼" thick; if they're thicker, it will take longer to bake them and the cookies may taste a little of flour.*

*Arrange on a parchment-lined or greased cookie sheet, one inch apart. Pre-heat the oven to 350 degrees F and bake for 8 – 10 minutes or until lightly browned. Remove from the oven and let cool for a minute or two before lifting them to a cooling rack. The recipe makes about 40 cookies.*

### Decorating Options:

*Before baking, sprinkle the cookies with plain sugar, coloured sugar, or fancier crystals available at cake supply shops. You can also press a few finely chopped nuts, bits of coconut, or dried fruit into the cookie dough. Or you can make a little hollow in the middle of the dough and add a bit of jam or a couple of chocolate chips.*

*After you have baked the cookies, you could also add various colours of icing, or you could melt some chocolate onto the cookies and even write your child's initials on them.*

*Special thanks for this recipe go out to*
*Erin McArthur and Mike Gillan.*

I hope you have enjoyed several hours with a child while you were making Santa's homemade Scratch Cookies. There was probably some giggling and laughter. And I suspect that in years to come, this child will look back and fondly remember their day of baking in the kitchen with you. I daresay you'll have the same wonderful memories. Not to mention all of those fabulous cookies!

## Chapter Nine
### May I come with you?
### December 9th

few years ago, I had lunch with my mother at her condo in early December. At the time, she was 89. She asked how Santa's visits were coming along, and what my schedule was like over the next few days. I told her I had an upcoming visit to an elementary school and, to my surprise, she asked if she could come along. My first reaction was a polite "no." Bringing my elderly mother along was not exactly convenient. But I quickly reconsidered. How many more opportunities would she get to join me on one of these trips? So we agreed on the time when I would pick her up. I also explained how we needed to arrive about 30 minutes before the scheduled visit because my Santa outfit was in a suitcase and I needed to change.

The next morning was cold, with snow and northeasterly winds blowing in from the North Atlantic. I started my truck, turned on the heater, and found the little green step-stool so my mother could climb up into the cab. Then I headed out to the senior's building. As I pulled up under the canopy, there was my elderly elf, all dressed in her red coat, with a red hat, scarf, and gloves. I got out, placed the stool on the ground, and gently helped her into the truck. She was full of excitement. In fact, she said she had been thinking about the visit for hours. She waved to her friends who had come down to see her off on this little adventure. Then away we went.

It was still snowing when we arrived at the elementary school. Fortunately, a very caring principal met us at the front door. Mother was assisted into the building and taken to the auditorium, where they had a seat for her next to Santa's big red chair. Then I retrieved Santa's suitcase from the truck. Thankfully I was taken to a room that had a lockable door and a mirror. (I am not always that lucky.) The school staff told me I had about 20 minutes before I would hear the children start to sing "Here Comes Santa Claus." As usual, this was the cue to make my entrance.

When I opened the big case, there on top was the checklist of the 18 items that had been carefully packed. This list is critical. There is no room for error here, and with more than 30 visits a year, you must show up with all the parts! Soon the pants, boots, belly, and coat were in place. I added the glue and used the Velcro straps to secure the beard to my welder's skull-cap. Then the hair gets pulled down before the earphones and radio transmitters are turned on. I added the hat, prescription glasses, long white gloves, and the large-face watches for each arm (one set to local time and one to the North Pole time so that Santa can talk to the children about what the elves are doing 5½ hours earlier than the local time).

At this point I was almost ready to go, but I needed a few more details. The reindeer bells on a leather bracelet have to slide on over my right glove. Finally, the mailbag goes over my left shoulder before I attach my driver's license to the strap on the bag. (The children are amazed that Santa has an official driver's license, and so are their parents.) Then I heard the familiar melody that has introduced me more than 1,000 times over the years. I picked up the big green bag full of presents and I opened the door.

First there is a hush. Then there is gleeful delight as the children realize who has come into the room. The teachers work to restrain them, but I don't mind that one child has pulled off my hat and another child is hanging from my belt. I try to manage this attention, as I mentioned in a previous chapter, because I know that bullying is potentially a problem in any school. Some children are more assertive than others, so this is a fine line that can be easily crossed. Almost unfailingly, the teachers try to keep all children in their class under control. I "high-five" a bunch of the children as I move to my red chair.

The teachers are wonderful helpers as Santa gives out the treats that have been carefully supplied. We are very conscious of nut allergies, for example, so Santa and his helpers always follow the directions carefully laid out by the school. It is always fun when – from the back of the room – the class teacher holding a radio transmitter sends me a message. Through the headphones I hear, "On your right, Santa, in the blue dress is Helen. Her sister's name is Julia, and they just moved here from Calgary."

Santa waves and turns to Helen. "Hello, Helen. Welcome to St. John's. Santa saw you and Julia last year in Calgary. It is nice to see you again now that you are here in Newfoundland."

Oh, how I wish I had a camera at that moment! Their eyes are wide, their faces shine, and their mouths drop open in disbelief. How did he know?!

Soon the teachers ask if the children have questions, and Santa is handed a microphone. There are the usual questions about the names of the reindeer, how we get into a house without a chimney, do the reindeer poop, and how do we get all around the world in one night. All pretty standard questions for Santa after decades of school visits. Then one small child puts up her hand and I turn to her. My earphones crackle as I hear the name "Sarah."

"And what is your question, Sarah?"

She points to my mother proudly sitting beside me and says, "Santa, who is the old lady with you today?!"

Well, I am speechless! So I turn the question around.

"Who do *you* think the lady is here with me today?"

Finally a voice says, "I think the old lady is Santa's sister." There is a joint "Yes" from the group, and everyone agrees she has to be Santa's sister. Soon the alarm goes off on Santa's North Pole watch to remind us it is time to go back home. We wave goodbye and I find my way back to the security of the change room. I carefully take out the checklist and place the items back in the case in the exact reverse order, all the while checking the list twice. Soon, Santa is secure. Then, an ordinary man pulling a suitcase moves out into the crowded school hallway and closes the door. My mother gives me a big hug and she is still laughing. We get her into the big truck to head back to the senior's home.

As we pull up to the door, her friends all ask how Santa's visit has unfolded. Mother regales them with her story of Santa's Sister. I know she must have told the story countless times over the holiday season.

I believe we only get one chance to make a memory for a child, but there are days when that phrase can be expanded. On one special December day, we made a memory not only for a mother, but a mother (now deceased) made a memory for her son. That happy experience will be remembered forever

Merry Christmas, GG. I miss you.

Chapter Ten
May I have this dance?
December 10th

The Gathering Place is a centre in downtown St. John's where people can find warmth, a hot meal, and an atmosphere of dignity and respect. This shelter is supported by two Roman Catholic parishes and three Anglican parishes, although it is operated by the Sisters of Mercy Congregation and the Sisters of Presentation. All of the activities take place in a former school that has been converted for this mission. For five days of every week the Sisters serve their "clients" – and it is a monumental task. With the help of many volunteers, they make sandwiches, large pots of soups and stews and wash endless dishes. These guests also get a haircut if they need one, as well as clothing, and even books to borrow. Imagine entertaining more than 150 guests in your house from Monday to Friday and you will get the picture.

These people are not homeless, but many are from rooming houses in St. John's where they may not be able to cook.

Sometimes they have very little money to pay for food because their meagre income is spent simply keeping a roof over their head. Many of the guests suffer from depression, dementia, or other forms of mental illness. On a shelf in the room where Santa changes for his visit, there are brochures on the shelf: *The Care of Scabies* and *How to Cure Ticks and Lice*. I realize this is the room used by a retired nurse who does volunteer work with the nuns. These are obviously just a few of the challenges involved in ministering to the needy in difficult times. I ponder these things as I get ready for my visit, and I remember an earlier conversation about those challenges.

Santa had a meeting with the nuns back in October when we talked about a visit to the Gathering Place and the task of preparing a full Christmas dinner for the guests. Santa asked one of the Sisters if some of the elves at the Rotary Club could provide Christmas hampers with a turkey or ham, potatoes, carrots, and a box of Christmas biscuits for each of her 150 clients.

"Oh my, no!" was her reply. "Most of these people have no place to cook. And even if they did, many are not capable of making a meal."

"Well, Sister, could you answer this question. What gift would make it a very special day for your guests? Santa could then see what he could do." The nun's reply came as a complete surprise.

"Santa, if all of these people could wake up on Christmas day and wash with a clean face-cloth and a bar of nice soap, and then dry with a clean soft towel, it would make all the difference to them. If they could brush their hair with a brush and comb and clean their teeth with a toothbrush and toothpaste, it would make a great start for their day. And then if they could put on a warm T-shirt or undershirt, together this would be a huge gift for all of them."

Well, Santa was thunderstruck. Most people in the developed world take all of those things for granted. On Christmas morning they would be up, showered, shampooed, shaved, and possibly sitting with children opening presents and stockings – without any thought at all to hot water, a towel, a toothbrush, or a bar of soap.

"Sister, if Santa could arrange 150 such packages, would that be a big help for your clients?"

"Bless you, Santa, yes," the Sister replied. "There are 100 men and 50 women, and a simple package like that would make all of the difference in the world to them."

So Santa started calling his elves. Three of the local pharmacists canvassed their suppliers for the soap, toothpaste, and toothbrushes. Another call to a Rotary buddy in the beauty products business secured our 150 packages of shampoo. Then we turned our minds to the T-shirts. We remembered that another Rotarian was in the business of selling monogrammed golf shirts, so he seemed to be a good person to call. Yes, he had 150 lightweight T-shirts left over from the summer. Then he asked why we needed them. We described the plight of 150 people who live in cold rooming houses, along with our plan to give them something special for Christmas. His tone got even brighter, and we were reminded of the saying that the Lord sometimes works in mysterious ways.

"Why didn't you tell me that is what you were going to do?" said Rotarian Dave B. "In December, my showroom is full of the old line of ski jackets, ski pants, Ski-Doo suits, and parkas. In January, I will get a whole new line for the new season. Why don't I box up the showroom samples and send them over to you?"

The next day, a truck arrived with 17 very large boxes. Soon after, the employees of a local engineering firm all went to work using 150 large, strong, double-handled Christmas gift-bags. Into each bag went all of the hygiene products. Then we topped them up with complete suits of outdoor winter clothes. A local grocer (yes, another Rotarian) heard about what the elves were doing, and he sent over 150 boxes of chocolates and 150 boxes of biscuits.

And so it was that on the appointed day, at the requested hour, Santa and his elves arrived at The Gathering Place. Dinner was over, and the sound of Newfoundland's most famous band could be heard throughout the building as we walked down the hall.

"They must have a copy of the group's new CD in the sound system," said one of the elves to Santa. But we were wrong. As we entered the room, yes, everyone was dancing. But we were bowled over to see Alan Doyle and *Great Big Sea* with the nuns and guests and bishops and clergy all dancing to the most wonderful rendition of "I'm A Rover, A Rambling Rover" and "Here Comes Santa Claus."

When the music stopped and our truck had been unloaded, each of the guests came forward and was given an enormous bag. Some of them untied the ribbon to take a peek inside. When they saw the beautiful fleece-down jackets and pants, many started to cry. It was a moment that none of us will ever forget. Even though Santa sees how "behind the scenes" things get done, he still cannot fully explain some of the outcomes.

Later in the spring, I met one of the Sisters from the Gathering Place. She told me about her wonderful dance with Santa, and how their guests all had the warmest Christmas they had ever experienced. She said she hoped Santa's trip around the rest of the world had been just as rewarding.

I was not sure how to answer. Santa's work pales in comparison to the work of these wonderful nuns. They have more powerful friends than all of Santa's helpers put together.

Angels surely watch over the Gathering Place.

The Christmas Tradition of Santa Claus
Part Two

It takes a very big leap to get from this saint in Eastern Europe in 350 A.D. to the modern Santa Claus we know in North America. What was it about St. Nicholas that caused such fascination? It helps to look at the world through the eyes of people during those dark and often violent times. They did not have the benefit of modern science to explain everyday life, so they often turned to the mystery of a Supreme Being to give them answers. Here is where St. Nicholas took on such special significance.

People were looking for a direct link to this Supreme Being, and patron saints became part of that connection. Religious figures such as St. Nicholas were thought to be intercessors or "advocates" for people of the faith. These saints could offer help to those in need. They were supposed to be God's "assistants" on Earth – usually capable of performing actual miracles. St. Nicholas, as we have already learned, was believed to be especially helpful to sailors in their time of need. But people in other crafts or professions also claimed him as their special intercessor. The long list of those who held him as a patron saint included scholars, pilgrims, soldiers, and even shoemakers.

Sailors carried stories of St. Nicholas on their travels all over the world. As a result, chapels with his name were built in many seaports. When his popularity continued to spread during the Middle Ages, he became the patron saint of Apulia (which we now call Italy), Greece, and Lorraine (now known as France), as well as many cities in Germany, Austria, Switzerland, and the Netherlands. St. Nicholas was so widely respected that thousands of churches were named for him, including 300 in Belgium, 23 in the Netherlands, and more than 400 in England. Today, you can even find a little bit of this tradition in Newfoundland if you visit St. Nicholas Anglican Church in Torbay.

As part of this dedication to St. Nicholas, the church dedicated December 6th as a special feast and celebration, when stories of his goodness and generosity were recounted. In Germany and Poland, boys would dress up as bishops to beg alms for the poor. In the Netherlands and Belgium, St. Nicholas used to arrive on a steamship and ride around on a magnificent white horse giving out gifts.

December 6th is still the main day for gift-giving in Europe, although the eve of that day is also an important time for celebrations. In the Netherlands, for example, candies are hurled at doors, and chocolates are made with the initials of children's names. Dutch children even leave carrots and hay in their shoes for the saint's horse, with the hope that St. Nicholas will exchange them for small gifts. With all of these wonderful traditions, it is not surprising that many of them "emigrated" to North America and became part of our culture. St. Nicholas, the patron saint of sailors, came to the New World. And here, as we shall soon see, is where the story of St. Nicholas and Christmas really started to grow.

Chapter Eleven

Have you written your letter to Santa yet?

December 11th

Every year the children of the Sunday school classes at St. Andrew's Presbyterian Church in St. John's present the nativity play for the congregation. One year the minister turned to the congregation and asked for a show of hands as the rehearsals were starting.

"Raise your hand if you have ever played Joseph or Mary." About 20 hands went up.

"Who can remember being the innkeeper, a shepherd, or Herod?" Again, many hands shot into the air.

Yes, this is a long-standing tradition, but each year the performance still captures everyone's imagination. Joseph and Mary come down the centre aisle in their robes, which have been carefully hemmed for each child's height. The innkeepers sit quietly with their lamp, waiting to send Mary and Joseph to the stable. The three wise men arrive with their precious gifts. The position of Gabriel is always carefully chosen, because the three-and four-year-old angels all need a leader.

Even with all of the help and preparation, there is still pandemonium, with angels winging up and down the aisles while delighted grandparents and mortified parents all try to keep their budding Oscar-winner focused on the job at hand. The shepherds are guarding their flock and actually seem to have most of them under control. A wise producer has put a bowl of Cheerios under the fake campfire to keep them entertained. Then the narrators take us through the story as baby Jesus arrives and is placed in the manger. Sometimes his arrival has been abrupt, and he has actually landed on his head in the manger! But the story moves ahead anyway.

At the conclusion of the play, the minister comes forward to sit on the chancel steps. All the children gather around him so they can have a little chat. There is no rehearsal and no tape-delay to "bleep" a child if there is some spontaneous but perhaps awkward moment. What is said by the child comes directly through the speakers – to the delight and the horror of parents and grandparents.

One week in early December, the minister was talking to the children about the true meaning of Christmas. When he finished his five minutes with them and offered a prayer, he asked them a question.

"Do you have your letter written to Santa Claus yet this year?"

One child put up a hand and said in a loud voice, "No sir, I am going straight to God this year." The church erupted in laughter, leaving the minister speechless.

There are a variety of messages about the Christmas season. Our minister certainly knows about the donations we get for the food banks during the Santa Claus Parade, and he knows about Santa's visits to the Janeway. At the same time, he knows we need to keep the Christmas message in perspective. It is a question of finding balance. We hope to raise children with a very clear belief that Christmas is more about giving than receiving.

Maybe St. Nicholas is, in fact, coming back. There seems to be a quiet shift when it comes to setting the expectations for children. Some parents are pushing back at the notion that a child will get everything on his or her wish list. Some parents even explain that Santa needs help, and they encourage children to think about giving some of their gifts to others who are less fortunate. Santa has gone to Christmas parties where he has been asked to bring the big green sack with the gold tassels – but to bring it *empty*. The children are invited to bring a present that Santa can deliver to other children on Christmas Eve.

So, here is our prayer to St. Nicholas. Don't give up hope, because your message has not been lost. And may God bless the child whose Christmas letter has been sent directly to God!

Chapter Twelve
Why does daddy like to drink?
December 12th

When I first had the chance to be Santa Claus, I was given the opportunity to meet the special elves at the John Howard Society. Some readers may know that this organization does extraordinary work with inmates and their families. It is a tremendous support group for those who have stumbled at some point and been disciplined, but who now want to rebuild their self-esteem and confidence so they can return to a normal life. The John Howard Society does everything in its power to support the families of inmates as well, so one of the natural outcomes is a Christmas party for children.

In the early years of Santa's visits, the location of the children's party was known only to the staff. Taxis were actually sent to pick up the children and their parents, because there were potential security issues. Some of the prior offenders were under intense stress after their release from prison. Some of them were also separated from their spouses and children. In both instances, the safety of the children was very important. Even Santa was only told about an hour in advance where the party would be held – just to minimize the chance of an errant mention of the location. Fortunately, in all the years that Santa has gone to these events, there has never been a problem.

When Santa walks into the room at a John Howard Society party, there is usually a rush of little kids who come and wrap their arms around Santa's leg. One little boy once announced, "Where is the sleigh, Santa? I'm not going back to my house. I want to come back to the North Pole with you."

Staff members used to worry about Santa getting hurt when the children rush to greet him. After many years, the volunteers now know that Santa is completely comfortable with the children. It's okay if the children climb on his back, pull off his hat, or lie down on the floor with him while he hauls out *'Twas the Night Before Christmas* for the umpteenth time. That said, this room reveals a special group of children. I imagine an older brother or sister will be the one who brings the youngest child forward. Or it will be a hard-working parent trying to provide a "normal" Christmas while the other partner is incarcerated.

I do know that some children seem to be asked to carry a heavier load than others. One of those children has been visiting with Santa for the past 12 years. She arrives in a wheelchair because she has spina bifida. I am told her life expectancy may be affected. I also know her father has been in trouble with the law for most of his life, yet this adorable child with her curly hair has a happy disposition and a beautiful personality. She has even appeared on telethons for the children's hospital. A total believer in Santa Claus, she squeals, "Santa! Santa! Santa!" as she wheels her chair forward in the crowded room. With her mother's help, Santa lifts her from the wheelchair and puts her gently on the floor so they can have a special chat. I admire this young girl's courage.

There is another child in a similar position who asked Santa a very difficult question.

"Why does my daddy love to drink more than he loves me?"

Santa gave the child a hug. "I am sure your daddy loves you very much Julie, and I know he thinks of you every day."

"Oh, thank you, Santa," said this precious little girl.

"Santa, please tell him when you see him that I love him too," she said.

Then there was a situation where an adult was convicted of impaired driving on 18 occasions and was finally sentenced to three years in jail. An elf called Santa when she heard about this man's daughter and her special wish for Christmas. She wanted Santa to bring her "a used computer and an Internet connection so she could e-mail her dad in jail." Once Santa's elves had all of the details of this request, they went to work at the North Pole. The computer was not hard to find. Then a fabulous group called the Aliant Pioneers (a group of retirees at Bell Aliant) arranged to have her house hooked up before Christmas with Internet service.

For many years, my little friend in the wheelchair has gone home with Santa's Own Teddy. She is bright, cheerful, and loves life. Nothing breaks her spirit, and I have never seen her down or disappointed. She is a child I think about when I hear people complain about something trivial. If we could all just wheel a mile in her chair, I suspect we might see life very differently. Each year, I hope to see these children again, and I am grateful to all of the people who help make our visits possible.  It is groups such as the John Howard Society, the Rotarians, and members of the business community who come together to make sure that this child – and hundreds of others like her – receive the support they need.

Chapter Thirteen
Why are you here?
December 13th

There is a senior's home in St. John's that has a daycare centre on the lower level full of preschoolers. On the upper floors of the building, seniors are housed according to the service levels they require. All of the floors are cheery and bright. Over the years, Santa has made many visits that start with the seniors home and end with a visit to the daycare.

I enjoy visiting seniors. You can tell a lot from the pictures in their rooms. Some contain multiple photos of children, grandchildren, and great grandchildren. Other rooms have children's artwork with happy cards taped on walls and mirrors. Some seniors are completely at peace with where they are in the world. I still remember a blind lady who I visited for many years. When I would ask "How do you feel?" she would give me the following response.

"I am well, Santa. I sit here by the window and feel the warm sun on my face. I smell the breakfast being made across the hall and I hear the laughter of the staff in the kitchen. I am at peace with myself and the world."

On one occasion, my blind friend was with her financial advisor and her son, who had power of attorney. They were assisting her with cards and presents for her family. I apologized for interrupting their meeting, but was invited into the room to answer a question. "Santa, is it better to give from a warm hand?"

What a beautiful question for a senior to ask! I had never heard it asked in quite this way before, so I offered a simple answer. I said it was her personal decision to make.

"Well, Santa, I can do this now or after I am dead; and now seems like a good time to me!"

Santa chuckled and gave a small bottle of sherry to this wonderful senior, because he knows she likes a little drop of medicine before supper.

Despite this woman's blindness, she has a very positive attitude towards life and lots of family support. But others are not as fortunate – especially if they suffer from dementia, which is a very cruel illness. Lots of research is being done on aging and senescence. Terms such as "telomeres," "cell division," and "the Hayflick limit" are coming into more common use as we all learn more about the limits of the human mind and body.

Santa sees the elderly in good health and those in poor health. He sees the bruising that comes from minor bumps, the diapers needed to deal with incontinence, and the frail shells that remain when people lose body fat and get weaker. Santa has also met many happy people in assisted living homes. They accept the reality of where they are. They are warm, secure, their food is prepared, and they accept Santa's cheery visit and a box of chocolates or some small treat. Yes, even a bottle of sherry!

But sometimes you get an unhappy surprise when you walk into a dreary room void of flowers or family photos. There is nothing on the walls, no photo of a current or past loved one. The senior sits in a dark corner and greets you with a defiant voice when you walk in the room.

"Why are you here, Santa?" It is hard not to be taken aback.

"I have come to brighten your afternoon, ma'am. What would you like for Christmas?"

"Answer this question first," she demands. "Santa is for children. Why do they treat me like a child in here?" I hardly know what to say.

"Christmas is coming. There must be something Santa could bring you," I say hopefully.

"Well, Santa, do this for me. Tell my son and daughter that I miss them. Tell them I am lonely, and I'm sorry that I'm bitter. Tell them I love them, and that more than anything in the world, I would like to see my grandchildren on Christmas Day."

These seniors do not ask for much. Medical advancements prolong our life expectancy, and more and more organs and joints can be replaced, but it is dementia, depression, and lone-liness that are still difficult to treat. So, on behalf of this senior and many others, I am delivering their request. I have kept my promise and passed along their wish to their children.

As I turned to leave this lonely soul, I suddenly had an idea.

"Would you do Santa a favour and come down to the day-care in the basement and have a little visit with the children?"

She looked at me and scowled. "I might, Santa," she said, grudgingly.

So my elves and I proceeded through the remaining floors with the seniors and then headed to the basement. I waited in an office while the seniors who wanted to join us were seated in a large recreation room. The children were all dressed in their Christmas best, the tree was alight in the corner, and a teacher was leading a rousing chorus of "Here Comes Santa Claus." Then, on cue, Santa walked into the room and got down on the floor.

There was great excitement and curiosity as the adoring chil-dren rushed to see Santa to ask if he had received their letter. I looked up at the seniors, many of whom were smiling. Then, across the room and coming through the doorway was my sen-ior friend from the third floor, pushing her walker and seeming a bit shaken by all the noise and commotion. She found a chair and sat down.

Santa turned his attention to the children and the doling out of presents. They were all wrapped in beautiful paper, each package with its own candy cane and bow. One package had a fruit bar instead of a candy cane. Just then, a little girl piped up.

"Santa, I can't eat candy canes. They may have peanuts in them and I am allergic to peanuts."

"I know," said Santa. "That's why your present has something different."

Santa turned to pick up two apples from a table. He asked the little girl if she would like an apple now, so she could take the fruit bar home for later. She said that would be fine. Then Santa asked her if she would take the other apple and the bow-ribbon over to the lady with the walker. The red bow had a sticky backing on it. The child reached up and carefully placed the bow in the lady's hair. Then she gave her the apple.

At this point, the room had gone quiet enough for Santa to hear their conversation.

"Thank you, sweetheart. I have a granddaughter just like you. I hope to see her at Christmas. Would you like me to read you a story?"

As Santa waved goodbye a little later, a cheery wave came from the senior and her new friend sitting on her knee. Santa went back to the North Pole to tell Mrs. Claus of his latest adventure. As usual, this brought a smile to her face.

To all the parents with children and to those of you who are still fortunate enough to have your own parents, Santa's Christmas wish is that you might share your children with those who love them and may be missing them – particularly on this special day. This is a gift that might be truly priceless.

Chapter Fourteen
Can you hear me?
December 14th

*L*ike many things in life, beginnings and the endings are the most challenging. For Santa, arriving and departing from an event is a challenge, too. The easiest way to arrive at a location is to have a pre-arranged time when a loud knock on a door signals Santa's entry to a room. Then, at the end of the visit, you ask a group of elves to gently hold the children back while you depart through the same door you entered. Or there are occasions when I arrive in my street clothes with Santa in a suitcase and the organizers have a change room ready so that Santa can appear at the appointed time. Sometimes, however, those departures can get complicated.

I visit a group every year that offers special support to families in distress. Sometimes drug or alcohol problems, mental health issues, or financial challenges may force a family to seek the help of a support agency. One such group meets in a church hall to host a Christmas party for the children of these families. Everyone gathers at 4:30 p.m., when an entertainer performs for the children. Depending on the year, it might be a juggler, storyteller, clown, or a musician. The children play games, sing songs, and everyone manages to forget their problems in a happy celebration. These are not your typical kids. Their clothes are often hand-me-downs, and the children do not have the fresh-scrubbed appearance you might see in a middle-class urban school.

There is one little guy in the community I will call Jason, and he and Santa have become friends. The youngest child in a family of four, Jason has three older sisters. His mother is a single mom with a loud, large, and sometimes forceful personality. Sometimes she swears at Jason in public, which makes the church minister cringe, but he has heard all of it before. There *is* such a thing as the verbal abuse of a child, and Jason sadly knows all about it.

Santa represents a very special person to Jason. When he sees Santa at two or three events over Christmas, he rushes into Santa's arms at every opportunity. He will actually push other children out of the way in order to wrap his arms around one of Santa's legs when he comes into the room. His mother sometimes slaps him on the back of the head, curses at him, or tells him not to be so rude. But I know the little guy is only looking for a male figure to trust, plus the reassurance that a hug can often bring. So, on every occasion, Jason gets a hug and the opportunity to take Santa's white gloved hand to lead him up to the Christmas tree and Santa's chair.

One time when I arrived at the event, I was told that a change-room had been set aside on the second floor. It had a mirror and access to a washroom, both of which made it the ideal spot. When I went down to the children's event, I took the room key and put it in the mailbag so I would know where to find it. After the visit, I waved goodbye to the children and headed for the door. Suddenly, Jason ran out the door ahead of me into the hall.

"I'm not going home with my mother, Santa," he cried in a very loud voice. "She hates me. I am going back to the North Pole with you!"

Fortunately, when I turned around, there was a volunteer heading over to pick Jason up. I figured I had better walk smartly toward the stairs to the second floor. I fished around in the mailbag until I found the key, but just as I got to the door I heard little feet pounding up the staircase. I opened the door, whipped inside, closed and locked the door, and turned off the light so nobody could see any light under the door. Although it was pitch-black in the room, I managed to find my suitcase so I could start to change into my street clothes.

At this point, I could hear Jason come down the hallway. He tried every door until he got to the room in which I had locked myself. Then I heard his sad plea.

"Okay, Santa, I know you are in there. Please open the door. I really need you."

In my suitcase, there is a hair-brush, an extra pair of gloves, extra double-sided tape, and a small flashlight, just in case. As I tried to get out the flashlight, I hit the top of the case with my right arm and the bells jingled.

"Can you hear me, Santa? I can hear your bells. I know you are in there and I'm going back to the North Pole with you."

At this point, I was stuck between the proverbial rock and a hard place. I wanted to comfort poor Jason, but I also knew he would be devastated if the magic of Santa Claus was taken away. I had to make the *very* painful decision not to disillusion this little boy.

Slowly and very carefully, I wrapped the bells – still on my arm – in the pillowcase in which I normally carry the hair and the beard. After I slid off the glove and the bells, I gingerly placed them in the case on top of the soft jacket. It took about ten minutes, but slowly I managed to get all the Santa parts back in the case. Then I retrieved my street clothes from the travel bag. All this time, I was painfully aware that a needy child was sitting outside the door. Soon I could hear his name being called by the volunteers. Then his mother chimed in.

"Jason, where the hell are you?" This was followed by other expletives. I heard a commotion outside, followed by the loud slaps of someone hitting a child. The little boy sobbed as he was led away. Then he offered this heartbreaking goodbye.

"I love you Santa, don't forget me Santa. Please come and get me at Christmas."

It took about 20 minutes for all of the parents to leave the building, at which point I quietly opened the door. On the floor, there was a piece of paper and a red crayon. On it were the words "Please save me, Santa. I love you. Your friend, Jason." He had even scribbled a phone number. I was heartbroken.

I went down to the kitchen where I showed the note to event organizers. They told me there were problems in the house and that Social Services had sent case workers to meet with the mother. Unless the mother committed an actual offence, however, it is difficult to intervene or remove the children. I wondered aloud if this note might make anyone change their mind.

In all the years I have done my Santa visits, I have never felt I let a child down – except that one night when Jason sat sobbing outside the door. I think of Jason a great deal. And I will always wonder if I made the right choice. As a young child, he had a tough beginning. I can only hope his story will have a happier ending.

Chapter Fifteen
How did you know I was a girl?
December 15th

$\mathcal{S}$anta always has special memories of his visits to the Janeway Children's Health and Rehabilitation Centre in St. John's, but they do require a lot of preparation. He asks his elves many questions before the visits. However, all the preparation in the world sometimes doesn't help when you get posed an *extraordinary* question.

One year, Santa asked Mrs. Claus to help get him *super*-organized. He knew there would be 150 children – spread over various wards and floors – all anxious to see him. The elves told him the age ranges of all these young patients. In fact, the hospital auxiliary staff even broke that down into the number of boys and girls and their age ranges.

This particular year, the event started with an afternoon carol sing in the atrium of the hospital. The choirs performed beautifully, doctors and nurses put on funny skits, and we all had fun. This was more challenging than it looked, because all of the hospital rules have to be carefully followed. For example, there are allergy issues about peanut-free cookies, candy, and perfumes. Santa also knows his hands need to be disinfected between every ward, and especially between every baby held in the neo-natal unit. Because Santa comes in contact with so many children, the rules have to be even *more* carefully observed by the hospital's special guest.

Once the sing-a-long was over, we started on a tour of the different wards and sections of the hospital. The ladies from the Janeway Auxiliary had filled Santa's bag with the pink-wrapped and blue-wrapped packages, which were all coded for age ranges. Each child was going to receive an appropriate gift that had been approved by hospital staff. So, off we went with a portable keyboard strapped to a medical cart as we sang "Here Comes Santa Claus." Everything went as planned through the Intensive Care ward and the Burn Unit. We got through Infectious Diseases and the Isolation Units, too. Santa's organizational system seemed to be working flawlessly. Mrs. Claus was going to be so happy to hear about this visit when Santa finished his day.

When we reached a big door for the Oncology Unit, Santa was told there were twelve  children from age six to twelve who were receiving treatment for cancer. Not surprisingly, this can be pretty emotional for Santa, because he has grandchildren. It is hard not to think about your life and all the things you have to be grateful for when the big door swings open. The nurse called out, "Look who is here!" Sitting on pillows in the colourful playroom were twelve little children all as bright as can be. They were having a pillow fight, and there had been gales of laughter just moments before we walked into the room.

The room was beautifully decorated for Christmas and the pillows were all multicoloured. The thing you really notice is that the children have sparkling eyes, broad smiles, and bright white teeth. Then you remember that the chemo treatment has taken all of their hair. Usually, no one has bothered with wigs at this stage. This decision might come later, if and when they are discharged. In the meantime, these children are so natural that they accept the stark reality of the situation. However, one year there was a young girl preparing to go home from the hospital, and she was being shown how to use a wig. With impish delight, she spun the blond wig around so the long hair was in front.

"Look, Santa," she bellowed. "I'm Tina Turner!"

Once all the giggling and laughter was over, someone asked the question on everyone's mind.

"Hey, Santa, do you have any presents?"

Santa looked down to the big sack with the pink-wrapped and blue-wrapped boxes. Suddenly, there was a moment of panic. The pink-wrapped presents were for the girls, and the blue-wrapped presents were for the boys. How could Santa tell the boys from the girls, especially when they had no hair? Then you realize that some wonderful elf has anticipated even *this* little detail. A nurse in the doorway quietly tells you through your headphones each child's first name. Now Santa can say "Hi, Isabella" as he hands her a pink package, and "Merry Christmas, Jonathan" as he hands out a blue package.

But life is never this simple, especially for a sensitive young child.

"How did you know I was a girl, Santa?" Isabella asks when she is handed her gift.

Santa pauses for a moment, smiles, and then speaks in a half-whisper.

"It's magic, Isabella. Merry Christmas."

The Christmas Tradition of Santa Claus
Part Three

It turns out that the Dutch and German colonialists who came to North America several centuries ago kept the feast of St. Nicholas alive. In fact, Nicholas was declared the patron saint of New York in 1804. And here is where the story really starts to grow.

Washington Irving, the famous American politician, joined the New York Historical Society in 1809. When Nicholas had been made the patron saint of the city five years earlier, he was also honoured as the patron saint of the Society. Irving subsequently wrote a book called *The Knickerbockers' History of New York* in which there were many references to an "elfin Dutch burgher with a clay pipe" – which was Nicholas. Roughly a century later, in 1923, Clement C. Moore is believed to have written the now-famous poem first called "A Visit from St. Nicholas." Biographers of Moore think he was strongly influenced by Washington Irving's portrayal of St. Nicholas. That poem, of course, is now universally known as "'Twas The Night Before Christmas."

That is *part* of the curious history of Santa Claus. But how did we get from an "elfin burgher" to a big, bearded man in a red suit? Apparently we have a German-born artist named Thomas Nast to thank for this transformation. Nast was a political illustrator (cartoonist) who joined the staff of *Harper's Weekly* to serve as its war correspondent in 1862. In 1889, he was asked to assemble a collection of his Christmas drawings that had appeared in the paper over the previous 27 years. The book was called *Christmas Drawings for the Human Race*. Many of the five Nast children were used as models, and they were part of the imaginative scenes that in-

cluded "Santa's workshop" at the North Pole. The illustrations are adorned with holly and mistletoe, and with charming depictions of the toys of the day: a jack-in-the-box, hobbyhorse, toy soldier, and a doll with a china head and a sawdust-filled body.

At this point, we have the "person" of Santa Claus, along with elves, a workshop in the far North, reindeer, and the notion of flying around the world on Christmas Eve delivering gifts to children. Gone was the thin bishop with the miter cap and the other religious elements. But we are still far from the image of jolly old St. Nick. Then, in the early 1920s, a new Santa evolved.

In 1921, the advertising agency for Coca-Cola began using illustrations from an artist named Haddon Sundblom. It was Clement Moore's description of St. Nick that led to an image of a warm, friendly, plump, and human Santa. This Santa Claus was rotund, with a long white beard, and the iconic fur-trimmed red suit with a wide black belt and a big brass buckle. He also wore big boots. For the next 35 years, all of the Coca-Cola print commercials (and some of the ones on early television) portrayed Santa Claus as we have come to know him. And it's not just people in North America who have adopted this tradition. Santa Claus has been "exported" all over the world.

The modern Santa Claus has come a long way since the fourth-century Bishop of Myra. As we will see later in this book, some of the elements of Nicholas's life have been preserved and others have faded with history. Either way, the notion of a giving and caring Santa remains strong in the hearts and minds of true believers, both young and old.

Chapter Sixteen
Are you God, Thanta?
December 16th

I t was almost noon on Saturday morning when a group of children were finishing their dress rehearsal for the nativity play. The big performance was scheduled for the following Sunday, but the play still needed a lot of work. A frazzled volunteer teacher held her script tightly as costumes were removed in a hurry. A plastic baby Jesus had been left unceremoniously on his head in the manger. Mary and Joseph were racing up the main aisle headed for the door. Herod, the Wise Men, the animals, the innkeepers, and the angels all were in a rush to get next door to the hall for the main event.

The children had been told weeks in advance that if they were on time for the rehearsal, and if they were well behaved and had memorized their parts, there would be a lunch with pizza and soft drinks following their practice. More importantly, Santa would join them as well. So, upstairs in an elementary school classroom, Santa sat on a little chair waiting for the tap on the door to indicate it was time for his arrival. Soon he heard the click of heels on the tile floor, followed by a gentle knock.

"Okay, Santa, you are on!"

Santa stood up and lifted his mailbag full of candy canes carefully selected to be nut-free. Santa's big green toy bag was empty, but all of the children knew this in advance. As he rounded the corner to go into the hall, he could hear a guitar strumming and children singing "Here Comes Santa Claus." When he walked into the room, the children were seated on the floor in a horseshoe formation. Each had a wrapped gift in front of them, which they had brought from home. The teachers had talked to the children all about St. Nicholas of Myra. They learned about the work of Nicholas and why many of the pictures show him holding three bags of gold, three coins, or three oranges.

Once Santa was seated in his chair, the children came forward to place their gifts in Santa's green sack. The children told stories about their gift for a child somewhere in the world and why they wanted Santa to take these presents on their behalf. As each child came forward, Santa gave them a candy cane. Then he asked if they had a special question for Santa. One little girl named Anna came forward with her arms extended as she placed her gift in the bag. She had just lost her two front baby teeth, which she revealed when she flashed a big smile.

"Santa's wife, the tooth fairy, visited me last night and left me a present under my pillow," said Anna.

There were gales of laughter from her classmates as a great debate started over whether Mrs. Claus was indeed the tooth fairy. Then she turned slowly toward me and asked her question.

"Thanta, I do have one question. Are you God?"

Now Santa has a rule that he never lies. Nor will he ever brush off a child's question with the old trick: "Ask your mother or father." The question was there, the child was there, and an answer was needed, now!

Here is what flashed through my mind. How would St. Nicholas answer the child's question? As an Anglican Bishop, he was certainly better trained to answer the question than I.

But this was no time for complicated arguments, or theological distinctions. All this young girl wanted was her candy cane, her two front teeth, and a short answer to a (supposedly!) simple question.

"Well, Anna, Santa is just like you. I try to do something good every day. I love children all over the world, and I try to offer hope. I try to teach others to be generous and caring, just like you are doing here today. No, Anna, Santa is not God, but Santa is just like you because we both try to help God with his work."

"Sounds good, Thanta. Can I go now?" She jumped off my knee and ran back to her friends.

Maybe I had made things too complicated. Keep it simple, Santa. Keep it simple.

Chapter Seventeen
"Do you help big kids, too?"
December 17th

One day, Santa got an interesting phone call. I knew the caller, but I was not expecting her question.

"Hi, Santa. This is Karen, from Healing Expressions. Do you help big kids, too?"

Santa knows all about Karen and the wonderful work she has started. Every weekday morning, a group of adult artists meets with her for coffee. Together through art therapy, they try to transfer to the canvas all of the hurt, disappointment, and confusion in their lives. Through their art they find the compassion, courage, trust, and confidence to move forward with their healing. Instead of a fancy art studio, they meet in a Sunday school classroom in a local church hall. Karen, the organizer of this group, believes in the "holistic healing potential of art." In her little ministry, she offers this program to anyone who is grappling with mental health issues or addictions. Now she needed Santa's help.

Fortunately, Santa has an incredible group of support elves who can assist him with requests from people such as Karen. Sometimes that support comes through unsolicited offers. When I picked up the phone on another day, it was a busy oil executive who had been transferred to our city three years earlier. He was aware of my community involvement. He had also been listening to the local news. Earlier in the day, the police had found a body in the harbour. They believed the victim had died by suicide the night before. The man (let's call him Tony) was one of the artists whom I had known from Karen's art group. The oil executive asked a simple question.

"Santa, what does the community need? I want to do something."

"Give me five minutes and I'll call you back," I answered.

I phoned the executive director of United Way of Newfoundland to tell her about my caller's question. Our executive director knows what is happening with the charities in our province, so I was certain she was the right person to ask. She said I could mention the art group to the oil executive. I thanked her for her counsel and I called him back.

I told him the story of the art group. I explained, for example, that I had met one artist who told me she was "a cutter." When I foolishly asked what a cutter did, she told me she used a razor blade to cut her arms and legs. She said the physical pain hurt less than the depression as she struggled to deal with the death of her child in the aftermath of a fire. I knew morale within the support group was at a low point following the suicide and I told the executive about their situation. I told him the group really needed a lift — something tangible to help them in their therapeutic work. If they could get a single-lens reflex (SLR) camera and a laptop computer, for example, they could take photos through the four seasons. Then they could display those images on the screen as they began to interpret them on canvas.

"Okay, Santa," he replied. "Where do I find them?"

I was completely surprised by his question. I had merely hoped he would write a cheque to the group and leave it at the front desk of the oil company. I happily gave him the cell number for Karen at the art group. Then I went back to work. The next day, I got another call from an astonished art director.

"Santa, do I have a story for you!" said Karen.

She told me she had received a call from a generous donor who wanted to help her group. He and a friend drove to a nearby electronics store. There they bought a Nikon SLR and a laptop, a carrying case, plus all the requisite gear. Then he drove to the church hall where he met Karen and all of her artists. He unwrapped the packages and helped Karen set up the new system.

Karen was obviously very touched by this man's act of generosity. How many people go beyond the writing of a cheque and actually touch the personal lives of those in need? How many executives at the highest levels of multinational corporations would take the time to research and meet a community need? We all know it is so much easier to shy away from those who struggle with mental illness, fearing a world where we may come face to face with the depressed, the challenged, and the addicted.

"Yes, Karen, Santa and his elves help big kids, too, and not just at Christmas." But the real thanks goes to people such as our anonymous donor whose own heart was touched by a story of need – and who then touched the hearts of others in need.

Thank you Elf HP.

Chapter Eighteen
Do I have to sit on your knee, Santa?
December 18th

*C*hristmas breakfasts with Santa are a lot of work, but they are always fun. In order to serve pancakes, bacon, and syrup for these big crowds, it takes a small army of volunteers arriving at 5.30 a.m. to get the job done. It's always worth the effort. When you hear the squeals of happy children, you know you have all the ingredients for a memorable event. There are long banquet tables filled with adults and children, and even the occasional high chair. There is heat rising from kitchen griddles, with hair-netted volunteers beating flour, eggs, milk, and baking powder into lofty pancakes. As quickly as possible we get eggs, pancakes, bacon, and sausages loaded onto plates and delivered with juice to hungry, expectant children. The ever-familiar "Here Comes Santa Claus" music is playing, while volunteer helpers all decked out in red Santa hats and white aprons scurry like elves to make sure the event is a success.

Then, at some point, knowing that Santa is 30 minutes away, the call is made.

"We are ready, Santa. Come now."

One of my first Santa breakfasts took place many years ago at the YM/YWCA in St. John's. The breakfast started at 8 a.m., but Santa was to arrive in his helicopter at 9.30 a.m. The wonderful volunteers at the Y sponsored the event, while families were selected and invited by the Department of Social Services. For many of those who attended, this hearty breakfast did more than simply feed them.

Santa has been blessed with the support of many elves, including a wonderful aviation company (Universal Helicopters) that has shuttled Santa to children's event for many years. They pick up Santa at the North Pole, fly him to St. John's for his visits, and fly him home again at the end of the day.

There is an interesting series of sounds when a helicopter starts up. First, you hear the switches clicking as the pilot carefully goes through his checklist. Then, a starting motor begins turning the huge blade above your head.  At this point a throaty deep roar signals the jets firing up as you sit there bouncing and rumbling on the ground. The pilot checks his gauges while the conversations start with the control tower at the airport. Finally, we are given the signal to lift off, and this miracle of flight gently rises into the chilly morning sky.

We fly over the airport as we head toward the inner city.

On this occasion, we have received a rare permit to land in the middle of St. John's on a very small parking lot. Soon, we see the police cruisers with lights flashing at our location just as we start to descend. A red smoke flare gives the direction of the wind to help us line up as we come in to land.

Outside, the volunteers form lines with arms locked to keep the children safe. More than 300 children and their parents all stand quite transfixed behind barriers and the arms of the volunteers. Then Santa's chopper descends through the snow and blows clouds of snowflakes from the parking lot as the powerful blades gently put this magic sleigh on the ground.

Minutes later, Santa emerges to wade into the crowd. There are the usual little tough kids determined to prove that the old man is a fake as they grab for his hat and beard. So Santa stops and gets down on his knees. As he has done before, Santa asks the ringleader to come forward and he asks for the boy's help. He explains that Santa needs some bodyguards to get into the hall. Could this boy and his friends form a ring around Santa to get him into the building, up the stairs, onto the stage, and sitting in his big chair? The boy's attitude changes in a blink.

"Come on, guys. Santa needs a bodyguard," he announces as he takes hold of the big white-gloved hand and leads the way.

Soon, Santa eases himself into a big red chair on the stage while the next phase of the event unfolds. There is a photographer who will take family pictures, and we will do this for as long as it takes. An elf records the surname name and address, while the Y arranges to mail the photo to the family. There isn't necessarily any order to the lineup, but slowly the hall starts to thin out.

Every family is different. Sometimes the parents come forward. Sometimes the older brother or sister holds the nervous hand of a little sibling. Older brothers and sisters are wonderful helpers for Santa who do their utmost to keep the dream alive. When a large group is asked to come at the invitation of the Department of Social Services, Santa sees a wide range of people. There are immigrant and refugee families looking to start a new life in Canada; and there are families whose breadwinner may be between jobs and they need a little assistance this year. Santa can see that the third or fourth child is wearing jeans with patched knees, while some of the little girls' dresses are clean but frayed and worn.

On this occasion, it was all going well when a single little girl cautiously came forward. She was alone, with her mother seated at the back of the room. She was about four, with long blond hair in curls held in place with Santa barrettes. She wore a tattered pink dress and her face was downturned. She was very hesitant as she came forward. The elves all encouraged her to have her picture taken with Santa.

Santa leaned forward and said, "Hello, there. My elves tell me you are Annabelle and that you would like a Barbie Doll for Christmas."

Slowly she lifted her head and she looked into my eyes. Her face was blue with bruises. She had marks on her arms, as well. When I asked if she would like her picture taken, I held out my big white gloves to pick her up.

In a quiet whisper, she looked at me and said, "Please, sir. I'll stand beside you for the picture, but do I have to sit on your knee?"

Of course, we followed her wishes. Annabelle stood for the picture, got her present from Santa, and quietly returned to her mother.

Sometime later, Santa's visit ended and the volunteers and the few remaining children took Santa back to his chopper. The big blades started to turn as Santa strapped on his seatbelt before giving a thumbs-up to the crowd. The pilot looked carefully around him. Then we lifted into the sky. Even at a distance, I could see Annabelle waving from the doorway of the building.

Santa will never forget meeting you, Annabelle. You are now a grown woman and perhaps a mother yourself. I hope your life today is happier than when I first met you as that shy little four-year-old girl.

Merry Christmas, Annabelle.

Chapter Nineteen
Will you hold my baby Amanda?
December 19th

When the young woman approached me with a small baby wrapped in a pink blanket, my first thought was that this was an older sister bringing her sibling for a visit with Santa. Then she asked me a question.

"Santa would you mind holding my baby Amanda?"

After Amanda's mother sat on my knee for a photo, I asked if I could hold the baby for a few more minutes. The little child snuggled into my big warm red coat. Soon she fell fast asleep. I sat and rocked in the chair, happily humming "Santa Claus Is Coming to Town." About ten minutes later, the young mother came back.

"Santa, I'm going out for a cigarette. Can you hold onto Amanda for a few minutes longer?"

"Sure," I replied. I couldn't help but notice how pale the woman's skin appeared in this light. Her face seemed gaunt.

As she walked away, I looked across the room. We were in a church hall with about 50 other mothers and infant children. There were no other men in the room. There was a happy buzz as volunteers set out trays of healthy fruit, muffins, and a warm breakfast for their guests.

Santa was visiting the Healthy Baby Club, which is part of a larger group called the Brighter Futures Coalition. Its mission is to promote the well-being of families by providing services for parents of children from birth to age six. The Club provides support, nurturing, and guidance to pregnant and new mothers through volunteers who are designated as "Resource Mothers." Through these caring individuals from the community, the young mothers are given help in birthing and raising children – some of whom may be in medical distress. Infants who weigh less than 5.5 lbs. (2,500 grams) at the time of birth, for example, may have serious health problems. Some of the mothers may live in poverty, be under personal stress, or they may be single or socially isolated. I was told that most of the mothers in the room were, in fact, single mothers and many of the children were low birth-weight infants. Brighter Futures is a wonderfully supportive organization with nurses, nutritionists, social workers, and other support staff to help these young mothers.

When I looked at the sleepy little elf resting in my arms, I could see red pockmarks on the baby's face. At this point, a support volunteer came over and stood beside me. Quietly, and ever mindful of the privacy rules, I gently whispered in her ear.

"Does the baby have measles?"

"No, Santa. It is an issue we are dealing with," she replied. Then she leaned forward to explain in a quiet voice.

"Our young mother is 15 and the marks are because she is addicted to a new drug called OxyContin." (This was a few years ago.) "We don't know much about it yet, but we are working with her to resolve the issue."

There are many occasions when Santa visits an organization where he is asked to sign a confidentiality agreement, and for good reason. No names or personal information should ever be disclosed without the consent of the individual and the organization. Those who come to these support organizations often face great needs, and I am thankful for groups such as Brighter Futures for the extraordinary work they do in these circumstances.

Children do not pick the families into which they are born. At the same time, we must not judge those with addictions. Santa certainly has no special answer in these situations. I only know that on a sunny Saturday one day in December, a precious infant lay in my arms sound asleep. I also know that a very young mother was getting loving and professional help from an organization that comes face to face with every social problem imaginable.

In the years since I first saw Amanda, I have sometimes found myself asking a young child a simple question whenever I meet someone named Amanda.

I look in their eyes and say, "How old are you?"

Every time I see a name badge that says "Amanda," my mind flashes back to that church. Sometimes the child will answer in a way that makes me stop and reflect.

"I'm seven, Santa, why?" Then I think of the infant I held seven years before.

Where are you now, Amanda? Santa would love to know you are warm and loved, and he wants to wish you Merry Christmas once again.

Chapter Twenty
*When is it Christmas for you?*
December 20th

Santa always has a busy schedule in December, with many special events to attend and tight schedules to keep. But Santa also knows that children may have multiple Christmas parties on the same day. The results are stressful for everyone. I remember the response from a slightly frantic mother once when a child wanted to stay a few minutes more to ask Santa a question. It was late in the party, and this harried mother had the child's coat in one hand and the car keys in the other. She called across to room to her child.

"Come on, Sarah, we have to go! You don't have time for Santa now. We need to be at the next party in ten minutes." The child resisted.

"But mummy, I need to ask Santa a question." To which her mother responded, "Come on, Sarah. There will be *another* Santa at the next party. You can ask him your question when you get there."

Ouch! That kind of answer is tough on Santa. Sarah looked disappointed, too.

"But mummy, this is the *real* Santa from the parade, and I have an important question to ask him."

Sarah's frustrated mother grabbed the child, took her arm, and forcibly pushed it into the sleeve of her coat.

"*Now*, Sarah. The car is running and we have to go."

Santa watched quietly as little Sarah was ushered from the room. A minute later, I saw the taillights of a large, flashy black car roar past the glass door with a little girl waving from the rear window.

As it happens, Santa's next visit was about ten minutes away. He went to his truck, called ahead to his next destination, arranged to be met by an elf at the front door, and confirmed that all the presents were ready in a big green sack. When Santa pulled into the parking lot, there was a similar flashy black car, and Santa thought about little Sarah, who had been hastily ushered out of the last party before she could even ask her question. Santa went into the room ringing his bells and greeting the children with his usual "Ho, Ho, Ho! Merry Christmas!"

And what to my wondering eyes should appear but little Sarah!

"Hi Santa, nice to see you again."

Now there was time for her to ask her important question.

"Santa, when is it Christmas for you?"

This same question came up a few weeks after Christmas when I attended St. Andrew's Presbyterian Church in St. John's. The minister began her sermon with a question.

"When is it Christmas for you?" she asked the congregation.

My mind flashed back to the persistent young lady at two Christmas parties who had finally gotten to ask her question. So let me now answer it honestly.

Sarah, Christmas for Santa comes in many forms. It comes early in December standing at the top of a sleigh in the Santa Claus Parade when I see all of the donated food piled high on a truck. Mrs. Claus and I are thankful that almost 50,000 pounds of food and $20,000 has been brought by children and their families to share with those in need.

Christmas comes for Santa when he hugs a child and holds a newborn baby in his arms.

And it comes on Christmas Eve when we start on the Surgery floor of the Janeway and then go through Pediatric Intensive Care, the Neonatal Unit, and the Emergency Department of the children's hospital as we try to spread some of the joy of the Christmas season.

It comes again when Santa calls a nurse's house and says hello to her children. And again when I go to a seniors home, where they ask for a dance with Santa and a hug. It comes at a large kitchen shelter for street people run by convent nuns as they feed 150 guests who may not have the money or the ability to look after themselves. None of us knows when we may find ourselves in similar circumstances.

Christmas comes for Santa at an event for those with mental and emotional disorders who are doing their very best to find understanding and fulfillment as they work through complicated issues.

And, young Sarah, Christmas came for me this year when, for some unexplained reason, I had the wonderful privilege of meeting you twice in one afternoon – and having the chance to consider your thoughtful question.

"When is it Christmas for you?"

For readers, I invite you to join me in pondering this simple question and considering how we all might answer young Sarah.

The Christmas Tradition of Santa Claus
Part Four

As we learned earlier in our story, it was largely due to the advertising agency for Coca-Cola and the illustrations of Haddon Sundblom that we have our modern icon of Santa Claus. For 35 years, the soft-drink company showed Santa with a bottle of Coke and the 1929 slogan, "The pause that refreshes." More recently, polar bears seem to have overtaken St. Nick, perhaps because the company wants images that are less associated with particular cultures and traditions. Change is inevitable.

Some of those changes make it possible for a modern Santa to help keep the dream alive.

The tools of a modern Santa, for example, certainly keep the children in wonder. Two-way radios make it possible for specific children to be referred to by name, even at a large event. Even though Santa can arrive in a helicopter, children seem to be perfectly happy with the explanation that the reindeer are resting for their big trip around the world. A GPS makes it easier to get to the locations on time, while BlackBerrys, iPads and other electronic marvels allow Santa to move through his busy schedule with multiple visits each day. Velcro keeps major parts of his outfit in place, and carefully sourced yak hair helps create the closest approximation to Santa's own beard.

All of these modern conveniences help us keep Santa alive as a symbol and promise of the future. We can then do our best

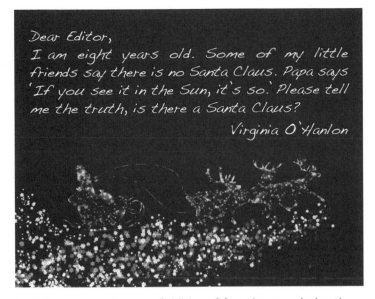

Dear Editor,
I am eight years old. Some of my little friends say there is no Santa Claus. Papa says 'If you see it in the Sun, it's so.' Please tell me the truth, is there a Santa Claus?

Virginia O'Hanlon

to deliver on the dreams of children. My only regret is that those dreams have become so focused on presents – and frequently more on *receiving* them than on giving them. But, as you have seen in many of the narratives in this book, often those gestures do not need to involve great expense. Some, in fact, cost nothing at all. Presents should be seen in the same light as Santa: a symbol of giving and caring.

Francis Church was an editorial writer for the *New York Sun* who received a now-famous letter from eight-year-old Virginia O'Hanlon and responded on September 21st, 1897. Virginia asked the question on the minds of many children.

"Please tell me the truth, is there a Santa Claus?"

Francis Church subsequently wrote the editorial that has been quoted ever since in response to her question. He offered the answer all of us who assist Santa repeat year after year.

"No Santa Claus?! Thank God he lives, and he lives forever," replied Church. "A thousand years from now, Virginia, nay, 10,000 years from now, he will continue to make glad the heart of childhood."

Santa in St. John's, Newfoundland, shares the opinion of Francis Church and millions of other believers around the world.

"Yes Virginia, there *is* a Santa Claus."

Chapter Twenty-One
Will you just look into her eyes?
December 21st

Santa works with some special elves who are very busy on Christmas Eve, but for different reasons. The professional staff at the Janeway Children's Health and Rehabilitation Centre keep long hours, regardless of the day or month. But they still share Santa's dream that every child must be visited on Christmas Eve. And every child means *every* child. Some readers may know that Santa has a "chief elf" at the hospital – a pediatric cardiologist who is also on call for the Intensive Care Unit. Yes, Santa's daughter is Dr. Christina Templeton. For many years we have done hospital rounds together on Christmas Eve. It is an absolute privilege to have my doctor daughter guide me through my visit.

One Christmas we were walking down a hall when we got to a door with warning signs all over it. This was a strict isolation unit. Because the patient was vulnerable to airborne disease, utmost care had to be taken. Signs cautioned us about proceeding into the unit without sterile clothing. Gowns and masks were essential. Quiet was requested. There were to be visitors only when accompanied by professional staff, and only one at a time. When you looked through the tinted glass, you could see that the lighting was subdued. But there were still coloured smaller lights flickering from various instruments, while IV stands measured the drip of solutions aiding a very ill but fortunately stable child. My daughter elf turned to me.

"Santa, we are going into the Burn Unit. If you just look into the eyes of the child, and nowhere else, we won't be carrying you out on the stretcher."

I asked what circumstances caused the child with the IV drip to be here. I was only told what I was allowed to know. The little girl was two years old – an Aboriginal child from a community in Labrador. When she went into a room in her home, she saw a flickering light on a table and wanted a closer look. So she pulled on the tablecloth. The kerosene lantern fell off the table and onto her head. When it smashed, fuel poured all over her. Within seconds her whole body was in flames. She screamed and a caring adult rushed into the room, grabbed a blanket off a chair, and rolled the child in it to extinguish the fire. The child was rushed to a local clinic, where she was treated for shock and third-degree burns.

The air transport team was then dispatched from St. John's to airlift her to the Janeway. At this point, specialists were using all of their skills to alleviate the pain and suffering of this tiny child. Now we were standing in front of her. It was Christmas Eve. There were no parents present yet, because they were still making arrangements to fly to St. John's. The child was alone, sedated, with bandages covering 95% of her little body.

Before we proceeded into the unit, the specialist on duty came to assess the risks of Santa going into the room. Evidently it was okay to proceed, but we would have to move cautiously so we wouldn't frighten the child. My daughter took the teddy bear we had brought for the girl as we opened the first of the two sealed doors into the isolation unit. When the first door was closed, she carefully opened the second door and went in, quietly whispering "Jingle Bells."

Two big brown eyes slowly opened as I went through the second sealed door. Cautiously, my elf waved me forward. Santa respectfully inched closer, gently ringing his bells and doing exactly as he was told. As promised, I looked only into the eyes of the child. Besides the bells and the beeping monitors, the only other sound was the pounding of my own heart. I had no idea what to expect.

When we got to the bedside and leaned forward, the little child's eyes were wide and glistening. Then, ever so slowly, a wide smile appeared. I am sure I heard a muffled giggle.

"Merry Christmas, sweetheart," said Santa.

My elf handed me the teddy bear with one hand while she held up a corner of the sheet with the other hand. With the doctor's permission, I put the teddy bear beside the child and we quietly left the room.

Chapter Twenty-Two
Will you move behind the incubator?
December 22nd

It is 9:00 p.m. in the Janeway Children's Health and Rehabilitation Centre and Santa is finishing his rounds of the various wards and some of the specialty units. We are in the Pediatric Intensive Care Unit (PICU) before we head for the Neonatal Intensive Care Unit (NICU) nursery. Within these walls are the sickest children in all of Newfoundland and Labrador, so sick they could not go home for Christmas. There are children in casts, some with IVs, and others with breathing tubes. One boy was shot in a hunting accident. One has suffered broken bones in a car accident, while another is in the terminal stages of cancer. While we are in PICU, a mother gently places her sleeping daughter into Santa's arms.

"Her name is Ariel, Santa. Could you hold her for a picture?"

This little elf doesn't stir while her candy-striped pajamas and Santa hat are adjusted by her loving but anxious mother.

I learned later that Ariel died on February 1st, 2012, and that the photo was shared at the funeral home. Loving parents, grandparents, relatives, and friends were all left to fathom the mystery. Ariel's grandmother spoke to me after I contacted them about this memoir.

"When your grandchild dies, your heart breaks twice – first for your grandchild but then for your own child as well."

So much sadness and pain on Christmas Eve, but there are no optional visits. Santa must visit every child – although I do admit a sigh of relief and gratitude as we head back out into the corridor from the PICU. I know the children are well cared for in this hospital. Everything possible is being done to help them through their trauma. It's just so hard to see children in such need.

"Come on, Santa, now we are off to the Nursery," my guide elf announces. We open the big yellow doors into the world of some young and potentially very small newborns. The Nursery is usually a pretty happy place. Santa has been in the unit many times already this year to have pictures taken with the babies. These nurses do a wonderful job of dressing the tiny elves in stockings, hats, and red and white striped PJs. (I didn't know they made candy-striped pajamas and red and green sleepers so small.) Santa gets to sit in a rocking chair as the children are brought to him beside the Christmas tree.

Usually, there is at least one set of twins and possibly triplets. There is a great breadth of weights and lengths, with children ranging from a tiny 570 grams to whopping 10 and 12-pound babies. Each of them is gently brought to Santa. This is a happy time. It is amazing how the children snuggle into the warmth of Santa's arms. More often than not, even a restless child soon settles down, and the nurses all comment on how content these precious elves are as they rest and quietly rock with Santa in his chair.

Once all of the children who can be transported have had a visit with Santa, I know it is time to move further into the unit to visit the children in the incubators or the ones too sick to be moved. The whole world here is different. There is a hush in the unit while some mothers sit rocking in chairs next to the incubators that hold their tiny children. There are wires and tubes coming in and out of the incubator, with heat, humidity, and oxygen levels all carefully monitored. Sometimes, the nurses ask Santa to sit in a chair next to an incubator. Then, when the hospital staffer is ready, the nurses turn up the sides of the incubator as a small child is gently lifted from the unit and placed with Santa. Tubes are very carefully tucked under little blankets for the photo as Santa looks in disbelief at the tiny elf in his hand.

"How small is this one?" Santa asks.

The nurse looks at the chart and says, "Just less than 600 grams, Santa."

Santa looks at the miracle and reflects on the hundreds of children he has held over the many years he has made Christmas visits. The technology over the past 30 years has changed dramatically. With a great team of caring professionals, it is now possible to give this tiny elf a fighting chance for survival.

"Will you come this way, Santa? We need another photo."

In a quiet, darkened corner, doctors and nurses are caring for a *very* small child. I see little wrinkly hands and a red face. The doctors and nurses tell me this child was born only an hour before. Then, Santa is asked to go behind the incubator to get down to the child's level. The hospital nurse knows exactly what she is doing and why this is important. Through the clear plastic incubator, the smallest child I have ever seen lies on a tiny mattress with a little blanket covering its fragile frame.

"No bells, Santa" says the doctor. "Just wave."

"Oh, Santa, we need to do this in a hurry."

I know not to ask why. I look around and see no parents or relatives, so I can guess the reason. The baby weights less than a pound and is 16 weeks premature. While the miracles get smaller every year, not all of the children survive.

The hospital has a procedure used when there is an infant death. Both the PICU and the NICU are equipped with a quantity of small wooden boxes which they call Memory Boxes, into which the staff places an assortment of items. There is a list with the names of the doctors and other professionals who were present at the time of death. A sheet with the names of the clergy and their contact information is also placed in the box, along with details about support agencies. There may be the little crib blanket, the tiny bracelet from the baby's wrist, a lock of hair, handprints and footprints, and perhaps the sensory monitors that had been attached to the child. And, yes, there is the photo with Santa.

The Memory Box is important for the grieving mother, father, and family. Over time they will likely go through the difficult stages of denial, anger, depression, and acceptance that have been written about so thoughtfully by experts such as Elizabeth Kubler-Ross and others trained in this area. Acceptance is an important part of the grieving process, which is why the photo with Santa is one of the special items in the Memory Box.

This is all part of the privilege *and* responsibility of being Santa. Visiting the intensive care units of the hospital on Christmas Eve for the parents, the nurses, and the children is one part of what it means to be Santa Claus. Yes, there are the parades, visits to the malls, and countless parties. But there is so much more to Santa's ministry. It is the visits with those in need that remind us of the many blessings in our own lives.

Chapter Twenty-Three
Will you ring your bells?
December 23rd

The parents of a young girl named Chelsea wrote a heartfelt story about their visit to the Janeway on Christmas Eve. They have graciously allowed me to share her story – and my perspective on that story – in this memoir.

Santa was doing his rounds at 9:00 p.m., while outside it was gently snowing. In one hospital room, the scene was quiet and serious. Chelsea's mother, Kim, sat on one side of a hospital bed and her husband, Barry, was on the other side. Doctors and nurses were all attending to this little girl lying almost lifeless on the bed. There were sensors wired to her chest. Her breathing was shallow and very carefully monitored.

Before I entered the room, I had the thought that my presence might not be appropriate, but you can never be certain in these circumstances. So, I always follow the wishes of the professionals. If the family did not feel I should be in the room, the staff would advise us before we entered.

One of the doctors looked up as I approached the bed.

"Oh, Santa, Chelsea cannot see you. But if you gently ring your bells, she may be able to hear them. She has had a seizure and is barely responsive."

Here, I would like Kim to report what happened. She wrote this narrative in a Christmas letter she later sent to friends. I include it here with her permission.

*"On Christmas Eve morning, I experienced two Christmas miracles in the matter of an hour. First of all, in what can only be called a Christmas miracle, Barry awoke and had enough sense about him at 6:20 a.m. to know that Chelsea was in serious trouble based only on the breathing that he could hear. Once he turned on the light, he realized that she was already well into a major seizure. He quickly woke me up and we gave her the emergency meds we have. Chelsea did not stop seizing so we took her to emergency where a team of about 15 doctors, nurses, X-ray technicians, lab specialists, and respiratory therapists took over 50 minutes and four additional shots of Ativan to get the seizure under control.*

*"It was here that I witnessed a second Christmas miracle, as even after 5 doses of Diastat and Ativan, Chelsea did not stop breathing. As a team worked on her, a respiratory therapist was standing at her head just waiting for the minute that she stopped breathing so that she could be put on life support. I could hear the nurses and the doctors commenting frequently that she should have stopped breathing by now and*

they were constantly warning us that she was going to stop breathing any second and that we should prepare ourselves. But she didn't. What else could it have been but a Christmas miracle?

"So now we found ourselves being admitted to the Janeway Hospital for Christmas – a place where you would not expect to find much Christmas spirit. But a place where Christmas becomes a lot more than a tree, presents, lights, and a turkey dinner! Here were the three of us without what I thought were the essentials for Christmas. I mean, I had spent weeks shopping, decorating, making plans, and sending Christmas cards, only to be in a hospital room without any of these things. I only had the things that were most precious to me – my husband, my baby, and the love and support of my friends and family.

"While in the Janeway, Chelsea was in isolation which meant that things going into her room could no longer be used out in the main part of the hospital and people had to be dressed in gowns and masks. The room was full of wires, breathing masks, and machines beeping, except for one big bright colourful blanket which hung over the head of her steel crib. It was a beautiful prayer quilt which had been made by members of the Conception Bay South Corps of the Salvation Army and had been given to Chelsea by two people who took the time out of their Christmas Eve celebration to come to the hospital and help us out. Christmas Spirit….

"As it started to get later on Christmas Eve, I began to think about all of the little kids who were anxiously awaiting Santa and about my baby who was lying in a crib very sick. Then, I heard Santa's bells. Can you believe that someone was actually kind enough to dress up as Santa and come in cheer up the sick children who could not go home for Christmas?

"I will never forget when he walked into Chelsea's room and the doctor said to him that Chelsea would not be able to see him, but if he were to shake the bells on his arm that she may hear them. As soon as he waved his arm, Chelsea opened her eyes and gave us a big smile!

"I guess that was Santa's present to me."

After Chelsea opened her eyes, there was a huge celebration in the room. This was the first time Chelsea had responded to anyone since her seizure almost 15 hours earlier. After a few minutes of a long, loving hug, a tearful mother stood up, turned, and hugged Santa very appreciatively.

Kim looked at me.

"Thank you, Santa. You have given me the greatest present you could ever give a mother. You have brought me back my daughter for Christmas. What more could a mother ask for?"

Chapter Twenty-Four
May I take a picture with Richard?
December 24th

I t is now 9:45 p.m. Christmas Eve, and this is our last visit of
the year at the Janeway Children's Health and Rehabilitation
Centre. Santa is holding up pretty well, but only because he is
assisted on these hospital visits by his chief elf. I am speaking, of
course, about my daughter. She is the confident professional you
would expect her to be, but she also knows how to prepare me
for what we might find behind the next curtain or door. I could
not make these visits without her.

The nursing and medical staff go out of their way over the
Christmas period to make sure every child that can go home is
given the opportunity to do so, even if only for a few days. So
Santa knows that those who are still in hospital are potentially
quite sick. Santa has gone to the Janeway on Christmas Eve for
more than 30 years. It is always a beehive of activity. On the
happier side, there are Christmas trees and stockings and lights
and presents. At the same time, there is the steady beeping of

heart monitors, the subdued lighting that provides a calm atmosphere, and always the look of prayerful and hopeful parents who sit in vigil beside a child in a hospital bed.

I treasure my visits to the Janeway and try to provide some moments of happiness. It is always fun to interact with the staff. I find a nurse with a young family at home and ask her to call her house.

"Jimmy, this is Mummy," the nurse says excitedly into the phone. "You will never guess who is standing here in the hospital with Mummy.  Can you hear his bells?"

She hands the phone to me and Santa rings his bells. Then Santa says, "Merry Christmas, Jimmy. Santa is in the Janeway seeing the boys and girls here, but I need you to go to bed right now because I am coming to your house next."

I don't know what it is like in Jimmy's house after that call, but I expect he is in bed pretty fast. One nurse called me after Christmas to report that her husband was up with their son until 2:00 a.m. because he was so excited. We have to keep the dream alive for every child.

Now it is time for Santa's last visit of the year. On the fourth floor, we go into the room of a young boy named Richard, who is lying on his side, peacefully asleep and wearing his Santa hat. He is about six years old, with his chin resting on his hand. Richard is wearing sports pajamas with a red number 32 sewn on his blue shirt. I am only told he is *quite* sick. Richard has a

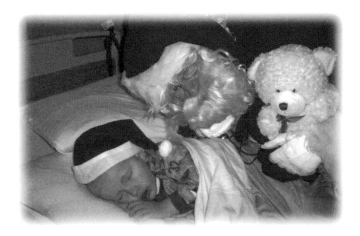

brain tumour, so the prognosis is uncertain. We carefully enter the darkened room, where Richards's grandmother sits quietly by his bed. I know his first name because it is written on the door.

"Oh, Santa!" she says. "Richard will be so disappointed. He just fell asleep waiting for you to come." Then she makes a simple request.

"Santa, would you put your head down next to Richard so that I can take your picture together? Then I can show him in the morning that you really did arrive."

"Of course we can," says Santa, and I get down beside Richard. Then Santa takes the last of the 36 teddy bears he started with in November and tucks it in beside the little boy.

The picture with Richard is beyond words. Santa has a copy. Richard's mother has it pasted on Facebook, because she has told the story of Santa's visit to the world.

This marks the end of Santa's visits through the wards, the Neonatal Unit, Intensive Care, Emergency, and Oncology. It is 10 p.m., so Santa's work is finished for another year. In an office on the third floor, Santa's red suit goes back into a big suitcase one last time. Christina and I leave the hospital, accompanied by the rolling sounds of suitcase wheels on the hard marble floor. The automatic outer doors open, the cold air hits my flushed face, and we walk toward our cars in the winter snow.

Chapter Twenty-Five
*Will you give your presence?*
Christmas Day

I clearly remember the year that Christina and I saw Richard, and how it felt as we walked out to the parking lot under a star-filled Christmas Eve sky. It was gently snowing. I turned to my daughter to ask her something that had been on my mind.

"Christina, I have been wondering. Do you think these Santa visits are still worth it? We have been doing this now for a long time."

She smiled and nodded. Then, two weeks later, she sent me an e-mail. The subject line was:

*An End to Wondering*

*Dad:*

*I don't really believe that you are still wondering whether going to the hospital on Christmas Eve is worth it, but just in case, don't wonder. Richard was beside himself with excitement when he woke up Christmas morning. His mother loves this picture so much she has had it enlarged. She gave me permission to send it to you. Two days ago he had a critical bleed, had emergency surgery, and is in Intensive Care. No matter what happens, this will be one of his family's favourite pictures forever. If he lives, they will show him the picture and tell him the story over and over for years. If he dies, they will remember him this way for the rest of their own lives. Either way, it was worth it.*

*Love,*
*Christina*

The hospital is a very private place, so I cannot be told anything about the children I see and hold. I rarely know surnames, nor do I need to know. I only know Richard's story because his mother has told it and given me permission to tell you. Richard died on December 6th, 2006. His mother wrote on a Facebook page that she plans to take Richard's picture with Santa out every Christmas for the rest of her life and place it on her mantelpiece. It is one of the last pictures taken of him alive.

I have promised my daughter I plan to be back at the Janeway again next Christmas.

Santa's journey is over for another year – but I have one more thing on my list. Actually, it's a request for you, my dear reader. Today, on Christmas Day, I would ask you to gently place your worries in a worry box and tuck them away until after New Year's. While you are doing this, you might also want to join me in turning off our cell phones and the other gadgets in our life. Together let us put our mind where our body is and be present in the moment with those we love. We need to use all our five senses to take in the experience around us. Now, let's store these moments in our memory to recall another time.

If you can, go for a walk in the snow. Make a snow angel with a child. Go sliding or skating and giggle and laugh. Put a marshmallow in a cup of hot chocolate. Make some sugar cookies from scratch with a child. Make pancakes in crazy shapes. Do a random act of kindness.

Remember the elderly and do anything that says "I care." Donate some of your time and talent to a charity. And, finally, in the quiet space of a sanctuary of your choice, and to any Supreme Being that you choose to have faith in, please join in giving thanks. For surely we are amongst the most fortunate people in the world.

I have had the good fortune to share precious moments with children for the past 30 years. Their stories and especially their *questions* have definitely changed my life. Many of those changes can be summed up in one sentence. *Christmas is far less about presents and more about presence.* The greatest present we will ever give is our own presence with our children and family as we create wonderful memories with those we love.

# Acknowledgements

A person does not set out on a 33-year journey (which is not over yet) and have it continue without a great deal of help and the collaboration of some very gifted people. I have seen how a publisher who took a leap of faith has been able to transform words into the finished book you now hold in your hands. Santa's helpers are numerous and generous. Here I am pleased to acknowledge my key elves.

First, I am grateful to my aunt, Miss Anna Templeton (1916-1995), without whom this Santa would never have climbed into that sleigh more than three decades ago. My wife Paula, of course, is given special recognition at the beginning of this memoir. My Santa adventures also involve my whole family, including my younger daughter Sarah, who has fetched and delivered Santa more than once. My son and business partner, Jim Templeton, and the other members of the JBT Financial Team have put up with a great deal of shenanigans in December when I am changing in the office boardroom before I go dashing out the door.

The Rev. Dr. David Sutherland at St. Andrew's Presbyterian Church has always shared my dreams for children. I grapple with where I should be on Christmas Eve, but he assures me that my ministry at the hospital is valid and important. Elf 342, Margaret Butt at Hallmark, has generously supplied Teddies for Santa to give away each Christmas for many years. The Rotary Club of St.

John's East (Elf SW) supplies milk and cookies to a whole school of elementary school children. The Naturals Group of the Rotary Club of St. John's supports Santa on many occasions. The Junior Chamber of Commerce (JCs) organization took Santa in his first parade on a freezing parkway in St. John's in 1978. The Rotary Club of St. John's Northwest was an early supporter of Santa's efforts. Craig Dobbin, founder of Sealand Helicopters, first flew Santa in 1979. Today, Universal Helicopters flies Santa several times a year. Provincial Airlines Ltd. and Steele Communications arrange for 18 children to fly to the North Pole to visit with Santa Claus. The Janeway Children's Health and Rehabilitation Centre and Margaret Tibbo go to great lengths to assist Santa in the hospital. To the medical and professional staff who are there (especially on Christmas Eve), thank you for allowing the visits to the children. And to my daughter, Dr. Christina Templeton, at my side year after year in some very tough situations, a very special thank you. You allow Santa to make a difference to those children and to some very worried parents who think that a hospital might be the last place they could be on Christmas Eve.

The City of St. John's and its support organization at Downtown St. John's organize the entire Santa Claus Parade. Gaylynne Lambert and Scott Cluney are owed a huge vote of thanks. The parade could not happen without the logistic support of the Rovers Search and Rescue. The employees of Newfoundland Power pick up all the food from the food drive in the parade, while Canada Post collects not only letters but financial contributions as well. Vogue Furriers and my wonderful elves at Custom Drycleaners, Laheys Hairstyling, and Embroidme are critical supporters who make sure that Santa is flawless in his lovely red suit.

Some of the history of Santa was completed with the assistance of Dover Publications, Inc., which published the wonderfully named *Thomas Nast's Christmas Drawings for the Human Race*. Quintet Publishing Ltd. in London published *The Story of Santa Claus,* and the website for The St. Nicholas Centre is a wealth of information about the life and work of this extraordinary saint. The Coca-Cola website tells the story of the images drawn by Haddon Sundblom.

My publishing journey has been a wonderful adventure. When I decided to take the story that had evolved in my head for more than 30 years and put it on paper, I happily found Creative Book Publishers (CBP) in St. John's. It was thrilling to get a call from the publisher, Donna Francis, to say they would share my dream with the world. This started a collaboration process that took just over 18 months to complete. My editor, Don Sedgwick, has been a critical part of that process. He took my rusty story and polished it into something beautiful and very special. Thank you, Don. Your ability not only as a wordsmith but as a coach through the whole process has been critically important. I thank Pam Dooley at CBP for her help with the marketing plans, and Josh Jamieson for guiding an old man through the social media of Facebook, Twitter, and author websites. These tools are all foreign to me – but essential to modern marketers.

I owe a final thank you to Danny Williams who took the time to read the manuscript while it was still in rough form. He called me on a memorable Sunday afternoon to endorse what I had started and to support all the efforts to see it completed.

We are not promised a tomorrow. All we can do each day is to behave in a way that we would want to be remembered. Rest tonight in the knowledge that you will be remembered because you were important today in the life of a child.

Santa

# Photo credits